Careers in Publishing and Bookselling

Careers in Publishing and Bookselling

How to get the job you want

Alison Aprhys

HALE
& IREMONGER

For Peter

First edition

10 9 8 7 6 5 4 3 2 1

Typeset by
DOCUPRO, Sydney

Printed & bound by
Southwood Press Pty Ltd
80–92 Chapel St, Marrickville, NSW

For the publisher
Hale & Iremonger Pty Limited
PO Box 205, Alexandria, NSW 2015

ISBN 0 86806 636 2

National Library of Australia
Cataloguing-in-Publication

Aprhys, Alison.
  Careers in publishing and bookselling: how to get the job you want.

  Bibliography.
  Includes index.
  ISBN 0 86806 636 2.

  1. Publishers and publishing—Australia—Handbooks, manuals, etc.
  2. Booksellers and bookselling—Australia—Handbooks, manuals, etc.
  I. Title.

070.50994

Cover design: Maria Miranda

Back cover photograph: John Brash, Fotograffiti

Contents

Acknowledgements

Thanks must go to the following people:
- Rhonda Black, Publisher at Hale & Iremonger for constant enthusiasm, encouragement, patience and support
- my Editor, Heather Cam, for valiant work, patience and her understanding
- Melinda Bufton, my wonderful Marketing Assistant, and the fabulous Monash Publishing Studies work experience students, Claire Haines, Sascha Jeske, Jo Lamborn, Morgan Mahoney, and Michelle Phillips (now at ACER), the CAE Bookselling work experience wonder Suzy Brunton, and the MLC work experience wonder Susan Ainsworth, for valiantly transcribing the taped interviews, collating data, keying in other essential information and making the best tea and coffee. (Any publishers wanting great publishing/editorial/marketing assistants look no further.)
- Susan Keogh for checking the chapter on editing and for providing timely suggestions and corrections
- Andrew Watson for assistance with the chapter on production
- Diane Carlyle for handling the index with professional expertise and care
- Susan Blackwell and Rina Afflitto, for assistance with industry statistics and information
- Emma Hollister, Ross Reading, Wal and Diane Butters,

Geoff Frost, Anne Richardson, Julie Maguire, Barbara
Cullen, Nick Walker, Leon and Peta Kowalski, Robert
Coco and Peter Klein for encouragement and enthusiasm
- Daphne Brasell, Bridget Williams and Theo Drake from
  Forresters' Books, all in New Zealand.
- all the people who kindly agreed to be interviewed, gave
  generously of their time and provided a marvellous range
  of information
- finally, to Bob Sessions, Publisher at Penguin, many
  thanks for suggesting I approach Hale & Iremonger as
  an appropriate publisher and for agreeing then to provide
  an interview.

N.B. Although much care and consultation has been undertaken in the writing of this book, details of courses,
addresses, and contact numbers will change.

Introduction

Publishing and bookselling are often seen as desirable industries in which to work. I've never met anyone who didn't like the idea of working in some way with books. At the moment, the book industry in Australia and New Zealand is going through challenging times — the advent of new technology has greatly altered the way books are designed and produced; the Internet and the changes in copyright have turned upside down the handling of intellectual property; due to our talented authors, designers, publishers, printers and illustrators, we are publishing and selling some of the best books in the world.

Although working in the book trade often presents a contradiction (never did I read so few books as when I was a bookseller, and when working in marketing, I had to promote as many books that I disliked as liked), the book trade is constantly dynamic and has lots to offer if you are looking for a diverse and interesting career.

This book aims to show the wide variety of positions that are available in publishing and bookselling, and to give you ideas on how to 'break in' to such a career.

In the chapters that follow you will find:
- information on publishing, bookselling, and related courses that are available
- interviews with people who recount how they made it

- tips from employers on what they are looking for in entry-level personnel
- how mature-aged people have transferred from another profession
- suggestions on putting together a publishing-friendly CV and writing a snappy and eye-catching cover letter
- suggestions on how to obtain valuable work experience
- a list of professional associations that can provide information
- a list of reference titles and recommended reading.

After sixteen years, the book trade is still, for me, an inspiring, interesting and stimulating industry to be in. I hope that this book encourages you to consider some of the wide range of career opportunities available.

If, after reading this book, you try some of these suggestions, please let me know how you got on. It is always great when someone I met through a training seminar or course or lecture that I've run, rings me up and says 'I've got a job at XYZ publishers or bookshop!' I look forward to hearing from you, and perhaps featuring you in the next edition.

Good Luck!

1 Industry background

What is the book trade? In Australia and New Zealand the book trades are industries that are wide-ranging, exciting, and full of opportunities. They embrace selling, marketing, publicity, editorial, production, repping and more. They involve turning a manuscript into a book that can be read, loved, hated, enjoyed. Books are still the best way to communicate ideas. The process of converting a bright idea into an item that is sold to readers with enthusiasm is complicated and involves the many skills that together constitute publishing and bookselling.

They are also highly competitive businesses where the books produced today must sell tomorrow or be returned to the publisher to be remaindered (sold off very cheaply), or pulped and recycled. They are industries that produce an enormous number of books and non-book products (think of all those CD-ROMs, book tapes, trade journals, and book reviews). In past times, it was enough for a publisher to produce and booksellers to stock books that were considered worthy but dull, or titles that had little or no market. Today, books are competing more and more with other items for the leisure dollar, as well as with books imported from the UK and the USA. While there are (bless them!) bookaholics who continue to read, love and purchase books, books must compete with videos, computer software, the Internet, and other items.

1

Publishers and booksellers

Publishers and booksellers rely on an array of different skills: finance, editorial, marketing, logistics, administration, information technology, retail, customer service and production are but a few. And there are as many types of publishers and booksellers as there are books and customers.

Australians and New Zealanders are fortunate to belong to literate countries. We are amongst the highest consumers per capita of books and magazines. We read everything from crime to craft to cooking; travel to textbooks; reference to romance; professional to performing arts; biography to bird-watching. We read anything and everything, everywhere (I will never forget seeing a sign in outback South Australia that read: 'Ice, Petrol, Books'), and in every format: the commuter reading a paperback on the train; the reader holding their large-print hardback book; the farmer listening to a booktape while driving the tractor; the student learning from a CD-ROM reference title. We are people who respect and love books and we publish and sell books that are up there with the world's best.

The reason that publishers and booksellers come in so many forms is that customers and readers also come in many guises. There are so many titles being published now, that both publishers and booksellers are focusing ever more closely on the customer, to ensure that the books they publish have a market and will sell. Market research is playing an increasingly important role as publishers are keen to expand their lists and booksellers their sales.

The Australian Publishers Association (APA) has over 150 members, and represents many (though not all) Australian publishing houses (companies) and New Zealand publishers belong to the Book Publishers Association of New Zealand. There are the big trade publishers who publish a wide selection of titles through many product categories. These include: Allen & Unwin, HarperCollins, Pan Macmillan, Penguin, Random House and Transworld. In New Zealand they are Penguin, Random House and Hodder Moa Beckett. Other publishers focus on a niche market (that is, on a particular, specialised, highly focused area), though they may also publish titles in more than one category. Niche market publishers include:

Academic — Australian Scholarly Publishing, Cambridge University Press, Deakin University Press, Melbourne University Press, Oxford University Press, Victoria University Press, Auckland University Press, Canterbury University Press

Business — McGraw-Hill, Pearson Professional, Prentice Hall, Woodslane

Children's — Eleanor Curtain, Greater Glider Productions, HarperCollins, Hodder Headline, Scholastic Australia, Mallinson Rendel, Waiatarua Publishers

Craft — Five Mile Press, Lothian Books

Educational — ACER, Addison Wesley Longman (Australia and New Zealand), Harcourt Brace & Co., HarperCollins, Macmillan, Mimosa, Nelson ITP, Oxford University Press, Reed Education

Feminist — Spinifex, Tandem Press, Artemis

Fiction — Allen & Unwin, Fremantle Arts Centre Press, Pan, Penguin Books, Text Publishing, Transworld, Random House (New Zealand), Godwit, Shoal Bay, David Ling

Health — HarperCollins, Hill of Content, Penguin

Indigenous — Magabala, Aboriginal Studies Press, IAD Press

Law — CCH, Federation Press, Law Book Company, Butterworths

Professional — Jacaranda Wiley, Woodslane

Reference — Cambridge University Press, Dorling Kindersley, Jacaranda Wiley, Melbourne University Press, Oxford University Press, Macmillan

Travel — Lonely Planet, Hodder Headline, Reader's Digest, Universal

(And this is only a small example of the types and ranges available.)

Just as there is a huge variety of publishers, so there is a
huge variety of booksellers. The Australian Booksellers Association (ABA) represents over 650 members throughout the
country. In New Zealand the membership of Booksellers New
Zealand is 530 members of which 470 are booksellers and
61 are publishers. Our booksellers have a reputation for
being informed, well stocked and friendly. They can range
from the independent bookseller in your strip shopping
centre (Books in Print in Malvern, Victoria; Coaldrake's in
Milton, Queensland; Devonport Bookshop in Devonport,
Tasmania; Shearer's in Gordon, New South Wales; Beattie &
Forbes in Napier; Blackmore's in Nelson) to the chain in your
shopping centre (Dymocks in Melbourne Central or
Whitcoulls, Paperplus and Bennett's in New Zealand), to the
hip and funky Gleebooks in Glebe, Sydney, and Readings in
Carlton, Melbourne, or Poppy's in Remuera or Time Out in
Mt Eden, to the second-hand and antiquarian Berkelouw's
in Oxford Street, Sydney, or outside Berrima, and Kay
Craddock's in Melbourne (surely the winner of the 'most
looks like a bookshop' trophy, were it to be awarded).

Opportunities

If you want to work in publishing and bookselling, then in
Australia the east coast holds the most opportunities, especially for publishing positions. Of course there are excellent
publishers elsewhere; in the west of Australia are Fremantle
Arts Centre Press and Magabala; in the north, University of
Queensland Press and Jacaranda Wiley; in South Australia,
Wakefield and Omnibus. However, 99 per cent of all pub-
lishing positions will be located in New South Wales or
Victoria. In New Zealand most publishing opportunities will
be available in Auckland, but Wellington also has excellent
publishers in Bridget Williams Books and Daphne Brasell
Associates, and Dunedin has Otago University Press and
Longacre, and Christchurch has Canterbury University
Press.

While the same generally holds true with booksellers,
there is more scope to work in regional areas. Freelance
work in combination with the use of fax, modem and email
enables some jobs in publishing to be located 'out of house',

and even interstate. Despite the increase in mail and Internet order outlets, booksellers generally have to work face-to-face with their customers.

According to 1995–96 Australian Bureau of Statistics figures on book publishers, 5583 people were working in publishing at the time the data was collected. This figure does not include freelance workers, unpaid volunteers or unpaid work experience people. If we include these people, and also look at the number engaged in related areas such as printing, reviewing, and the media, then the figures become more impressive.

It is widely rumoured that it is hard or next to impossible to break into the professional world of publishing and bookselling. Attend any writers' festival, literary event or book launch and stories will abound of people who found it too hard or struggled for years to get the job they wanted. Rubbish! There is always room for the person with ability, enthusiasm and a bit of experience. Getting that experience may take you down a slightly different path, but, who knows, it may be one that you enjoy. Take the editor who wanted desperately to edit fiction. Her first editing position was working on non-fiction. She was given a book about insects to edit, and became passionately hooked on science titles. Since then she's been happily editing books about creepy crawlies, comets and conifers. Or consider the book-seller who wanted to be in publicity, took a sales rep's job to get a foot in the door, discovered a flair for sales and now earns lots more than the average publicist. Or how about the lawyer who hated being a solicitor and is now a copyright and permissions editor? Or the computer book-seller who became a freelance book trade computer consultant?

The book trade is made up of a myriad of opportunities — as many as there are books. Just keep your eyes and options open, your skills up to date, your enthusiasm high, and you are bound to succeed.

The interests of publishers and booksellers are pretty much the same: selling books to interested readers; readers who can be encouraged to continue to read and buy more books. Although they have this shared interest there can be real tensions between the two groups. For instance, book-sellers wanting increased discounts from publishers and faster turnaround of orders, and publishers wanting book-sellers to purchase larger quantities of new titles and to keep in stock titles that sell regularly (back list), rather than re-ordering when (and if) a customer requests it.

There is some movement of people across the two indus-tries and it might be better for all if there was the occasional swapping of staff. For instance, if editors spent a day or so on the shop floor really finding out what customers (book readers) want, and booksellers or reps spent time working with authors on their page proofs.

Both businesses are seen from the outside as glamorous: neither is particularly so. Publishing tends to be mentioned in the media only when literary awards are made, or a new author has earned a large advance on royalties. Neither of these represents the daily business that is publishing. For instance educational publishing is one of the largest sectors in publishing, but we don't commonly see such books on the shelves or reviewed in the mainstream media.

Both publishing and bookselling are becoming increas-ingly 'feminised' with some companies employing mostly female staff. Although management of the larger publishing companies still tends to be male, there are many successful female-owned and female-headed companies.

Many of the people in management in publishing and bookselling are highly skilled in their areas of expertise, though may not have management qualifications. They are often the baby-boomer generation and may be employing younger people who, on paper, have better qualifications. These managers are often people who 'fell into' publishing and bookselling and have all-round experience in their areas of expertise. Some of the younger people applying for jobs in publishing and bookselling have degrees and certificates and have very clear ideas about exactly what they want to do. Both industries are quite small and it may be necessary to take a circuitous route to your dream job. Like others before you, you may find you're good at, and enjoy, what you do along the way.

The management structure isn't always clear or structured in publishing and bookselling, and promotion within a company may not be in a logical, sequential fashion. However, they're both industries where people move between jobs and companies in order to expand and develop expertise, and this movement of staff isn't seen as a problem to potential employers.

Traditionally many have aspired to the role of editor, without knowing much about what it involves. There aren't necessarily sufficient editorial jobs for those initially wanting them, however, with the increased professionalism in publicity, promotions and marketing, those editorial skills you've spent time honing can be put to very good use.

The future

The book trade in Australia and New Zealand is going through enormous change. Issues such as changes to copyright (moral rights and parallel importing) and changes to book bounty (subsidy paid to book printers), improvements and growth in new technologies are all changing the way we produce and print books. Larger publishers take over smaller publishers; independents remain fiercely so, and publishers and booksellers come and go in an industry that is constantly dynamic.

The late 1990s are an exciting time for the book trade, and, although the idea of the book may change (is it printed on paper and bound, is it a CD, is it on the Internet?), the passion that goes into its creation and selling, will not.

Finally

In the rest of this chapter you will find:
(a) a diagram of the parts/roles that make up a publishing company
(b) an outline of the typical responsibilities for people in publishing companies
(c) a diagram of the parts/roles that make up a bookshop
(d) an outline of how bookshops (small, medium and large) are organised.

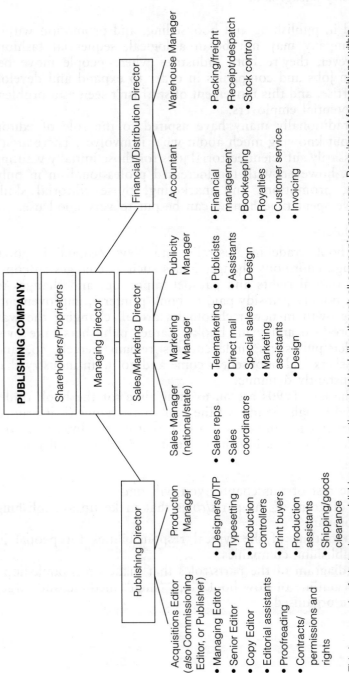

PUBLISHING COMPANY

Shareholders/Proprietors

Managing Director

Publishing Director

Production Manager

- Designers/DTP
- Typesetting
- Production controllers
- Print buyers
- Production assistants
- Shipping/goods clearance

Acquisitions Editor (*also* Commissioning Editor, or Publisher)

- Managing Editor
- Senior Editor
- Copy Editor
- Editorial assistants
- Proofreading
- Contracts/ permissions and rights

Sales/Marketing Director

Sales Manager (national/state)

- Sales reps
- Sales coordinators

Marketing Manager

- Telemarketing
- Direct mail
- Special sales
- Marketing assistants
- Design

Publicity Manager

- Publicists
- Assistants
- Design

Financial/Distribution Director

Accountant

- Financial management
- Bookkeeping
- Royalties
- Customer service
- Invoicing

Warehouse Manager

- Packing/freight
- Receipt/despatch
- Stock control

This is a sample of what a large publishing organisation might look like, though all companies may vary. Recruitment for positions within departments would normally be undertaken by the department manager, or, if a more senior role, the director, or managing director. In a smaller company one person would undertake several roles at once. Brief explanations of some roles follow.

Typical responsibilities for people in publishing companies

Acquisitions Editor
- Acquire manuscripts by commissioning authors, through literary agents, or unsolicited manuscripts
- Responsible for making and achieving budgets
- May be responsible for contracts/rights negotiations

Managing Editor
- Apportion work to editors and proofreaders, either in-house or freelance
- Responsible for day-to-day workflow
- Required to stay within editorial budgets and keep schedules
- May be responsible for allocating work to designers/desktop production

Senior Editor
- May carry out structural and/or copy-editing
- Will liaise closely with authors
- May brief or work closely with designers
- May do or commission picture research
- Required to stay within editorial budgets and keep schedules

Copy Editor
- Will copy-edit one or more manuscripts at a time
- Will draft back cover copy with author
- Will carry out proofreading
- Will check dyelines (film proofs provided by the printer)

Proofreading
- May be carried out by copy editor or senior editor or freelance editor

Permissions/Rights Editor
- Responsible for granting permissions requests (possibly also for seeking them); co-ordinating rights deals; possibly for generation of contracts and agreements

Production Manager
- Responsible for budgets, schedules and quality criteria being met
- Apportions work to staff, either in-house or freelance

- Oversees print or colour separation buying

Designer/DTP
- Responsible for internal design of books; may be responsible for cover design
- Responsible for desktop production formatting and/or typesetting prior to printing

Print Buyer
- Responsible for placing work with colour separators and printers
- Responsible for schedules being met
- May be responsible for shipping and clearing of goods if imported

Production Assistant
- May fulfil a coordinator's role or traffic control of proofs and parcels
- General clerical/computer support

Sales Manager
- Responsible for setting sales budgets and meeting them
- Responsible for running a team of sales reps, either in-house or commissioned agents
- Responsible for inventory control
- Liaison with marketing department to report on feedback from trade regarding new titles, covers and concepts

Sales Rep
- Responsible for meeting sales targets and budgets
- Responsible for selling books to bookshops
- May be responsible for authorising returns to publishers
- Responsible for liaising with editors about sales

Sales Coordinator or Assistant
- Responsible for liaising with managers and reps
- Responsible for gathering and disseminating sales materials
- May be responsible for producing point-of-sale material
- General clerical/computer support

Marketing Manager
- Responsible for meeting targets and marketing budgets

- Responsible for selling books and promoting the company, including advertising and point-of-sale
- Responsible for coordinating the work of the department, including telemarketing, special sales and direct mail

Marketing Assistant
- May undertake telemarketing, special sales coordination and direct mail
- May write copy for direct-mail brochures
- May be responsible for producing point-of-sale material
- General clerical/computer support

Publicity Manager
- Responsible for promoting books and authors through the media
- Responsible for increasing the company's profile with the media and the public
- Responsible for coordinating the work of the department
- Responsible for advertising

Publicist
- Responsible for gaining media exposure for authors; possible author tours
- Responsible for writing copy for the media
- Responsible for sending out review and other complimentary copies
- Will work closely with the author

Design
- Responsible for producing media releases, advertising, dummies, etc.

Accountant
- Responsible for coordinating the setting and meeting of budgets, cashflow and good financial management and planning
- Responsible for coordinating invoicing with warehouse despatch
- Responsible for bookkeeping; accounts receivable/payable; reconciliations; royalties
- Responsible for customer service for booksellers/general public

Warehouse Manager
- Responsible for timely receipt and despatch of goods
- Responsible for picking and packing
- Responsible for materials purchasing
- May be responsible for archival material from other parts of the company
- May be responsible for stock control

Note: Titles and responsibilities may differ between companies but the above list gives a good guide to the roles undertaken, and to the typical activity pattern in the production, publication and marketing of books.

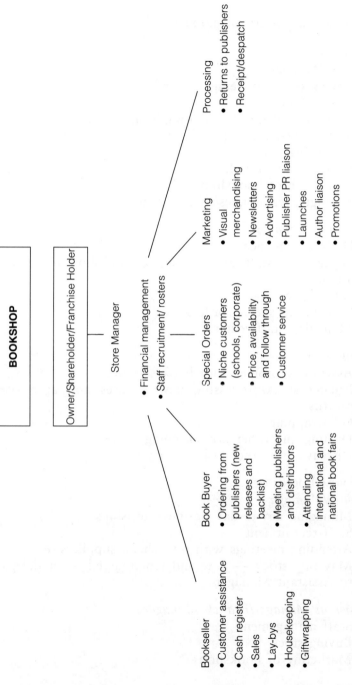

BOOKSHOP

Owner/Shareholder/Franchise Holder

Store Manager
- Financial management
- Staff recruitment/ rosters

Bookseller
- Customer assistance
- Cash register
- Sales
- Lay-bys
- Housekeeping
- Giftwrapping

Book Buyer
- Ordering from publishers (new releases and backlist)
- Meeting publishers and distributors
- Attending international and national book fairs

Special Orders
- Niche customers (schools, corporate)
- Price, availability and follow through
- Customer service

Marketing
- Visual merchandising
- Newsletters
- Advertising
- Publisher PR liaison
- Launches
- Author liaison
- Promotions

Processing
- Returns to publishers
- Receipt/despatch

A breakdown of the roles undertaken in different-sized bookshops follows.

Bookshop organisation made simple

SMALL BOOKSHOP
Owner/Manager
- Buying of stock/seeing sales reps
- Setting budgets
- Handling all legal/accounting/business matters; payment of accounts, chasing up invoices
- Reconciliations
- Recruitment of staff
- Marketing of bookshop
- Managing catalogues/special events

Assistant Manager
- Daily till balances
- Supervising staff and managing bookshop in owner's absence
- Sales duties
- Chasing up special orders
- Managing staff roster

Bookseller
- Assisting customer with book selection
- Pricing stock/processing new releases and authorised returns
- Giftwrapping
- Dusting and other housekeeping chores
- Displays and other tasks as required

MEDIUM BOOKSHOP
Owner/Manager
- Managing day-to-day business decisions
- Staff recruitment
- Attending meetings with publishers, suppliers, etc.
- May buy stock — new and remaindered — or delegate to Assistant Manager

Assistant Manager/Branch Manager
- Staff management
- Buying stock
- Marketing of bookshop

Bookseller
- Assisting customer with book selection
- Processing sales at the register
- Pricing stock/processing new releases and authorised returns
- Giftwrapping
- Dusting and other housekeeping chores
- Displays and other tasks as required

LARGE BOOKSHOP
Owner/Manager/Franchise Holder
- Managing day-to-day business decisions
- Staff recruitment and placement
- Attending meetings with publishers, suppliers, etc.
- May buy stock — new and remaindered — or delegate to Assistant Manager
- Marketing of bookshop
- Managing catalogues/special events

Area Manager/Buyer
- Management and buyer for specialist areas — i.e. business/children's
- Buying stock, organising returns
- Supervising staff and managing bookshop in owner's absence

Support Staff Area
- Processing — processing new and returned titles, despatching new and returned titles
- Special orders — hunting/checking price and availability
- Administrative — handling paper work/invoices, etc.
- Finance — managing budgets, accounts receivable and payable, wages, etc.

Bookseller
- Assisting customer with book selection in areas they are assigned — i.e. computers, travel, etc.
- Processing sales at the register
- Pricing stock/processing new releases and authorised returns
- Giftwrapping
- Dusting and other housekeeping chores
- Displays and other tasks as required

2 Bookselling as a career

How I started out . . .

It is surprising and reassuring to discover just what unlikely starts many successful book trade careers had. Here are a few samples:

'I started in a basement, sorting stock. I moved up to atlases, then globes, then poetry and then after about a year I went to the front of the shop . . .'
Bob Sessions, Publishing Director, Penguin Books Australia

'I arrived in Auckland jobless. I needed money. I saw a great ad: "No experience necessary, an interest in books preferred". It sounded like the perfect job to earn money to go overseas. I often remind myself of this when years later I find I'm still "hooked" in the book trade. Hooked because there is always something new being published. You are surrounded by the entire world in one shop from Bill Bryson galivanting off along the Appalachian Trail, Sara Henderson flying us into Bullo Station, Australia, to Witi Ihimaera showing us another side of New Zealand's education system. It's never dull.

'Dull . . . well there's still the housework to be done, dust, tidy, shelve. Better, there's book ordering. Re-orders are a challenge (how many can we sell this week if they arrive by . . .), while new titles are a bit of a lottery. Books can succeed or fail for the strangest reasons. The age of the "now" society can make life difficult as New Zealand is miles from every-

where and the Internet's lure is strong. But by being efficient, friendly, attentive and interesting, booksellers can keep the customers coming back.'
Kay Warburton, Dymocks, Auckland

'I never intended to become a bookseller, but as I am a compulsive reader, when the opportunity came to buy a bookshop, I jumped at the chance . . .'
Jean Ferguson, Book Industry Consultant

'I couldn't get a "real" job in 1978!'
David Gaunt, Co-owner of Gleebooks, Winner of the 1995 and 1997 Bookseller of the Year

'Although I didn't have any sales experience, I went in to the Melbourne University Bookroom, obtained an interview with Bruce, the manager, and when asked for experience, said, "I have worked for your trade division" (moving books at the MUP warehouse). Bruce said, "Hmm . . .", and so I spent the next two weeks in their basement, pricing remainder stock.'
Susan Keogh, Senior Editor, Melbourne University Press

'All through university I worked in bookshops, in fact I worked in a bookshop at school, during the school holidays . . . applied for a job at Harper & Row and I got the job because I had worked in bookshops.'
Susan Blackwell, Executive Director, Australian Publishers Association

'Technical Books is a family company, so I guess it's in the blood! I worked Saturday mornings dusting shelves . . .'
Caroline Radford, Managing Director, Sales & Marketing, Technical Book & Magazine Company

'We have operated our freelance book representation business from our home-base of Walton in Eastern Waikato, New Zealand, for seven years. We represent eight publishers and book distribution companies to bookshops and libraries throughout the North Island, except Wellington City.
  'Janet started in the book trade in 1981 working in the office of a publishing company. Within a year she was a sales rep travelling most of New Zealand. She spent nearly eight years with Whitcoulls, working in a number of stores as supervisor, book buyer, and store manager. She also was Whitcoulls Head Office Book Product Manager.

'Ross started as a publisher's rep in 1974. He has worked as a rep for six publishing companies and book distribution companies. After being a sales rep for a multi-national publishing company, he started their freelance business in 1990.'
Ross & Janet Miller Book Agencies, Walton, Waikato, New Zealand

'Definitely chance and luck played a part in my becoming a bookseller! The RAN College, Merchant Navy, clothing traveller, butcher, hunter, toy representative, then into book distribution and finally into book retailing is hardly a planned career path!'
Peter Milne, Deputy Managing Director, Abbey's Bookshops

'My first job was as a bookseller for the New Mint bookshop in Toorak. From there I worked for a variety of independent Melbourne bookshops for about ten years, and now I'm a sales rep.'
Julie Maguire, Sales Representative, Tower Books

'I walked into a bookshop, said I'm looking for a part-time job as I start at university next week. They rang me the next day and said, "Someone has resigned, can you start full-time on Monday?" I stayed a bookseller for ten years, and never did go to that university course.'
Alison Aprhys, Director, Bookstaff

Why I like being a bookseller . . .

Let's hear what satisfies those experienced in this area:

'It's very people-oriented, full of variety; there are as many different books as there are people. It can be a challenge (mostly a pleasure!) to help them find a book which you think they will enjoy.'
Meredith Horton, Co-proprietor, Pages Bookshop

'One of the exciting things about being a bookseller is unpacking the boxes and taking out the new releases!'
Anne Donnelly, Bookseller, Shelling's

'I love the autonomy and responsibility of my own bookshop.'
Barbara Cullen, Director, Page One

'I work in a business where children cry when they have to leave! One of my greatest pleasures is every morning opening

my bookshop's front doors. Any really good bookseller loves reading which is why we do it.'
Gail Mahon, Co-proprietor and Manager, Kidsbooks

Definition

According to most dictionaries, a bookseller is 'a dealer in books', but how narrow a definition is that! A bookseller can range from a part-timer at one of the bookshop chains (e.g. Angus & Robertson Bookworld, Dymocks), to a department manager in a large independent bookshop, to an owner–manager of a specialist mail-order book business, to a full-time sales bookseller position. The one common factor that should appear is a definite love of books and for dealing with people. There are several different types of bookshops in Australia and New Zealand, and all of them operate in a slightly different manner.

Bookshop types

Independent

As the name suggests, an independent bookshop is exactly that. Often owner-operated, some of the best bookshops fall into this category. In Melbourne, these include Readings Bookshops, Books in Print, Pages, The Avenue, Foreign Language, Technical Book & Magazine, McGills, Page One, Fairfield Bookshop and Cosmos.

In Sydney there are Abbey's, Shearer's, Pentimento, and Gleebooks.

Adelaide independent bookshops include Kidsbooks, Mostly Books, Pauline Books & Media and the AIM Bookshop.

In Queensland there are Coaldrake's, Mary Ryan's and Napoleons.

In Tasmania there are Devonport Bookshop and Fuller's.

Western Australian independent bookshops include Boffins and Awakenings.

Auckland boasts Unity Books, Parson's Bookshop (both also in Wellington) and the Auckland University Bookshop.

In Wellington there are Ahradsen's Bookshops and the Victoria University Bookshop.

In smaller centres there are Beattie & Forbes in Napier,

McLeod's in Rotorua, Muir's in Gisborne, East's in Christchurch, Bruce McKenzie Bookseller in Palmerston North, Blackmore's Bookshop in Nelson, Chapter and Verse in Timaru and Canterbury University Bookshop and Otago University Bookshop.

Company

Company bookshops are just that—owned and operated by a particular company rather than an individual, partnership or a franchisee. Both Angus & Robertson Bookworld and Collins also operate franchise (agreement between a company to a distributor or retailer to sell books under the company name, for a fee) as well as company bookshops. An example includes the famous Hill of Content, founded by A.H. Spencer in 1922, which in fact has been owned by Collins Booksellers since the 1950s.

Franchise

There are several types of franchise bookshops available in Australia: Dymocks, Collins, Angus & Robertson/Bookworld and Book City. The bookshops are available under a franchise scheme, whereby the owner pays a percentage commission to the franchise headquarters. By no means are franchise bookshops second best; an excellent example is the Angus & Robertson Bookworld Greensborough. This bookstore has exemplary staff and management, operating a friendly, attractive shop.

New Zealand has a system of bookshops linked under a brand name, but owned individually. Paperplus is an example where the shops will have the same name, be fitted out alike and have joint purchasing to give them purchasing power. There is also Paper Power, Top Line, and the Independents Group which doesn't have 'corporate' identification, but does joint purchasing.

Bookshop specialities

Trade

Trade bookshops sell general books or books that are available to the book trade. Examples are Readings (Vic), Gleebooks (NSW), Kidsbooks (SA), Pages (Vic), Abbey's (NSW). Trade bookshops traditionally have a wide range of titles and subjects and, while they do not have the range of a specialist store, often have a couple of areas that they may focus upon. For example, Hill of Content (Vic) is strong in literature and lifestyle; Pages (Vic) in children's and literature; Abbey's (NSW) in history, academic and business; Mary Ryan's (Qld) in literature and lifestyle; Coaldrake's (Qld) in literature and children's. In New Zealand examples are Unity Books and Parsons in both Auckland and Wellington.

Educational

Educational booksellers sell educational books: they may specialise in primary, secondary or tertiary titles and the accompanying stationery and software. Examples in Melbourne include Linehan & Shrimpton, Campion and North of the Yarra; in Sydney, The Textbook Agency and University Co-op; in Brisbane, The Language People; and in New Zealand, Schools Supplies.

Specialist

Specialist bookshops are niche-driven. They are often known as 'destination' bookshops, because people will travel or make an effort to get there since they will have a wider than normal range of titles in a particular subject area. Examples in New South Wales include: Galaxy (sci-fi and fantasy), Boat Books (nautical and maritime), Black Mask (crime and literature). In New Zealand there's the Women's Bookshop in Auckland, and Pathfinder in Wellington specialises in New Age.

Government

Government bookshops handle everything from Acts of Parliament and copies of department reports to maps and statistical data produced by a mind-boggling number of government areas. They often stock a range of relevant non-government material. Each state has an Australian Government Publishing Service (AGPS) bookshop. Other examples include the excellent Information Victoria and the Outdoor Recreation Centre for the Department of Natural Resources and Environment in Victoria. In New Zealand there's Bennett's Bookshop, Lambton Quay, Wellington.

Mail order

While most bookshops will have mail order as a component of their sales, there are some book businesses that are entirely mail order. An advantage is the saving of expenditure on fixtures, shop rent and costs, but by necessity, telephone, fax, email and Internet costs will be higher. Some examples include: NZ Books Abroad, Softback Preview and the Doubleday Book Club.

Internet

Probably the best-known bookshop on the Internet is amazon.com, based in Seattle, USA. Claiming a holding of 2.5 million titles, amazon.com also advertises for staff on its home page. Bookselling on the Internet is very similar to that of mail/fax order, however the home page must be updated each day, in order to keep the customers' interest. Just as a bookshop must change its displays of new and backlist titles, and mail order must regularly update their catalogues, so must a home page be updated too. On the day shown on the next page, August 26, amazon.com listed what titles were new on their shelves, titles in the news and their books of the day.

The vision

People often wander in to a bookshop, look around at the well-stocked shelves, soak in the lovely ambience of music, flowers on the counter, gorgeous new releases on display, the smiling booksellers, the happy customers buying, reading, browsing and discussing the books and say, 'I wish I worked in a bookshop . . .', or, with utter honesty and total naivety exclaim, 'It must be lovely to read books all day!'

The reality

In fact, bookselling is a very physical job. Unpacking, pricing, shelving books, creating displays, packing up orders or copies to take to displays, book launches or special sales can be both hard and dirty work. Dealing with customers is also a special skill. So many come in with a vague 'I heard about a book on health . . . it has a red cover' and expect the bookseller to know instantly the book they want. Or they can become annoyed (as though it were the bookseller's

Text Only

SEARCH BY
Author, Title, Subject
Keyword
ISBN
Advanced Query

BROWSE BY
All Subjects
Business
History
Science & Nature
Mystery & Thrillers
Children's Books
Religion
& Many More . . .

BUY BOOKS
Shopping Cart
Checkout

**VISIT OUR
SUPER ROOM**
Computer & Internet

FIND THE BEST
Bestsellers
Award Winners

READ REVIEWS
Expert Editors
Customer Reviews
New York Times
Oprah
NPR
Titles in the News

**READ ARTICLES
& EXCERPTS**
Amazon.com Journal
Author Interviews

HAVE FUN
Win Prizes
Want to Play?

**GET E-MAIL
ABOUT BOOKS**
Eyes
Expert Editors

PARTNERS
Associates
Publishers
Authors

AMAZON.COM
About Our Store
Press Clips

WELCOME TO EARTH'S BIGGEST BOOKSTORE

amazon.com

Browse by Subjects

Enter to win $100,000! ~ First-time Users Click Here
Join Associates and Earn up to 15% Selling Books
UPS Strike Shipping Information

~ New on Our Shelves Today ~

August 26th
With bad burgers, risky raspberries, and E. coli-laced sprouts, getting three safe squares is an increasingly risky proposition. *Spoiled* tells the tale of what's gone haywire with our food supply... Earn as you surf. Online investing is just a click away in the Computer and Internet Super Room... Plus, browse great titles in hundreds of categories and check out our Expert Editors' favorites.

journal . . . .

Amazon.com Journal: If you liked *Moo*, you'll love Richard Russo's *Straight Man*, a sharp send-up that literally gooses academic life... Publishers have recently released a flood of histories on World War II and the Holocaust. We consider the best of the lot... Bots are like cybertraffic cops with attitude. Should we fear them? *Bots: The Origin of New Species* says, "Be afraid." Read our exclusive interview with the author, Andrew Leonard, and the first chapter of *Bots*... We celebrate 50 years of Indian independence with fireworks from the nation's brightest literary lights... Books as tools for back to school... And *The Perfect Storm* is to the sea what *Into Thin Air* is to mountains. You must read this book.

Richard Russo

STRAIGHT MAN

Check out the Amazon.com Journal Table of Contents for articles, interviews, and more.

Titles in the News
Titles in the News: NPR considers Janna Malamud Smith's *Private Matters: In Defense of the Personal Life*, a lucid examination of privacy in the face of an American culture obsessed with 15 minutes of fame... The *New York Times* reviews Robertson Davies's *The Merry*

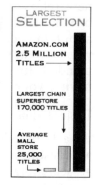

Books of the Day
Classic
Undiscovered
Science Fiction
Nonfiction
Mystery
Wacky

6 new books
every day
for the next
1,000 years

fault) if the title they request is out of print. The good customers more than make up for the difficult ones. You will never wear white, trousers are the norm for women because of the ladders they will have to climb and the immodest posture they will inevitably assume while unpacking, pricing, dusting, and reaching those hard-to-get-at titles and, if that isn't enough, sometimes the customers and publishers will drive you mad. Dealing with up to 40 reps a month is very time-consuming, but if you don't see their new releases, you don't know what the new titles will be or what to order. However, there is something very satisfying about unpacking the new releases, having a customer tell you how happy they were with the last book you recommended for them and would you suggest another, and having your customers turn into friends.

Typical duties

As a bookseller your typical duties will include:
- assisting customers to locate the books they want
- searching electronic and paper databases to locate these titles
- dusting and other household chores
- unpacking and pricing the new and back-order titles
- ordering new releases from the publishers' sales representatives
- arranging window and in-store displays
- contacting customers to let them know their special orders are in stock
- keeping up to date with all the reviews in the daily newspapers, literary and specialist journals
- attending to matters of finance—balancing the till, banking and reconciliation
- attending ABA meetings
- arranging promotions with publishers
- chasing up accounts and debts
- keeping up to date with international trends.

Career path

It used to be that many booksellers fell into their career by accident. Either they simply got a job while at university and stayed on, or they took it as a job while waiting for 'something better'. Other people took a job just because it was there, and have since been bitten by the bug. These days, a job in a bookshop is seen as an excellent way to get experience that will be very valuable as a step into a publishing position, and the competition for a first-time position can be fierce. Many people who want to one day run their own bookshop very sensibly decide to get a job working for someone else in order to experience what it would be like before committing themselves and their savings. As a bookseller, you can work your way up from a casual or part-time position, to become a manager of a franchise or company or your own independent bookshop.

Many people start out as a bookseller and then move into a publisher's sales representative's position. This is seen as natural career progression, as who better to sell books to booksellers than an ex-bookseller? Who better to know what booksellers want, what they don't want and how to assist them to sell more titles than someone who until recently was doing a similar job?

Salary

Salaries are not high. Many people who have the rose-coloured vision lose it abruptly when confronted with the paucity of the pay cheque. A full-time bookseller working 38 hours over six days generally earns between $A22,000 and $A27,000. The manager of a medium-sized chain bookshop might expect $A24,000 to $A28,000 and the owner–manager of an independent bookshop is looking at generally between $A35,000 to a considerable amount, depending on the success of the business. In New Zealand shop floor staff could expect to earn $NZ20,000 to $NZ25,000, whereas shop managers can expect $NZ35,000 to $NZ40,000 per annum.

Education level required

These days many booksellers have a range of qualifications, but most have successfully obtained positions with a Year 12 equivalent. It is true that many candidates seeking bookselling positions have had a tertiary education. A degree in literature is naturally enough seen to be a way in. Much more important, however, is your ability to communicate with other people—customers, staff, suppliers—and your interest in the books themselves. A love of reading will not get you the job, but a love of communicating your enthusiasm of books to people will.

Education that will help

The ABA runs an excellent distance education Certificate of Bookshop Practice. University and TAFE courses in literature and specialist courses on sales are also useful.

Booksellers New Zealand offer a correspondence course, 'Book Selling Certificate', in three stages. This course is for those within the industry who have some experience, but are relative newcomers. There is the option to do a fast-track course if the student has sufficient experience.

Skills that will help

You will more than likely need computer literacy, since most new bookshops and some second-hand bookshops are computerised for sales, inventory control, and so on.

The ability to sell is paramount. This assumes that you have people skills, that you get along with people and have a real desire to communicate and are good at listening to your customers' needs. It doesn't hurt to have the skills of a juggler. Being able to cope with customer requests, the bankcard machine, the telephone ringing while you are searching for an elusive layby without tearing your hair out will be much appreciated by any employer.

Organisational skills are important—booksellers typically have a lot to do in a short time.

3 Editing as a career

'My current position: senior publishing consultant, Harcourt Brace, reporting to the managing director. Responsibilities: publishing (or acquisitions) editor with particular area of front list; also managing production while the production manager is on leave, and consultant on various publishing and production matters.'

Penny Martin, Senior Publishing Consultant, Harcourt Brace & Co.

'What I love about publishing is the pathway from an idea to a set of pages in someone's hands. I go and talk to someone—an author, an academic, someone I don't know, a journalist. Three conversations later, and they're writing. They were probably writing anyway . . .Three years later—and I'm standing behind someone on the ferry, watching them turn the pages. An idea is out there . . . on the loose . . . someone's life has subtly changed. They've read a book. Sometimes I think it makes a difference that I was there, somewhere in the middle; often it doesn't really, I just gave witness to this delicious process by which the world moves on.'

Bridget Williams, Publisher, Bridget Williams Books/Auckland University Press

'I deal with the day-to-day administration of the department. I organise schedules, meetings with authors and editors and illustrators. There is a little bit of design work involved as well, working with the design department. I have to write copy for cover blurbs, and extra copy required inside the books. I

also write correspondence that my Editorial Director gives me, such as letters, some of which are routine, some are really quite complicated. So basically day-to-day administration, but since I joined last May, there has been increasingly more editorial work to do which is great.'
Jonathan Appleton, Editorial Assistant, Non-fiction, Scholastic Children's Books, UK

'What I wanted to do was be involved in the making of books.'
Carolyn Leslie, Editor, Non-fiction, HarperCollins

'For the first three months when I arrived at McPhee Gribble, I read the manuscript pile, and Hilary [McPhee] said I wasn't allowed to read ten pages or fifty pages and just give up, I had to finish every single one of them. And so for three months she sat me in front of the slush pile and I read. By the end of three months I knew exactly what was publishable and what wasn't; *all* of it was not publishable!'
Sue Hines, Publisher, Allen & Unwin

'I started off as a teacher and "fell" into editing for the education department.'
Louis de Vries, Manager, AGPS Victoria

'Editing found me! I've always enjoyed working with words.'
Deborah Doyle, Freelance Editor and Proprietor of 'Living Proof'

'I always had aspirations to do something in the literary field.'
Kristen Baragwanath, Acquisitions Editor, Schools Division, McGraw-Hill

'I think people have this ivory tower image that if you are an editor, nobody can bother you as you sit in your office all day and read beautiful prose. The best editors these days are people who understand the market and who can create a book or product for a specific niche.'
Alison Baverstock, Marketing Consultant

'I went into marketing because of my lack of ability to spell when I was a proof reader/assistant editor! Of course I didn't know it at the time, I just thought I was being promoted!'
Alison Aprhys, Director, Bookstaff

'You have to establish a good relationship with your authors

from the beginning, otherwise, no matter how great the book is, the project will be absolute hell.'
Anonymous Editor

'What makes a good editor—tact, tact, tact!'
Anonymous Freelance Editor

Definition

The editor is responsible for liaising between the publisher and author, for transforming the manuscript from an idea or concept into a workable manuscript on time and within budget. With only a simple or brief guide to work from, the editor must communicate to the author the publisher's vision for the book and communicate to the publisher the author's method for achieving this. Taking into account the original guidelines and advice from sales and marketing, the editor must work to see that the manuscript stays within the boundaries that will ensure the publisher ends up with the book that was intended, not something radically different. As well as editing the general text for the book, the editor may also be responsible for producing the cover blurbs, captions for photographs, illustrations and tables, indexes (which in themselves are a very specialised form of work), as well as the marketing notes that end up in the sales and promotions catalogues, flyers and media releases.

Editors are either in-house or freelance. In-house editors are just that, working within a publishing house on one or more titles as required, on a salary as an employee. Freelance editors may be working for a number of publishers on a number of titles at any one time. Freelance editors normally charge a higher rate because, as independent contractors, they do not receive the usual benefits of full-time employees, such as holiday or sick pay. Most freelance editors start out working in-house and then make the switch for one reason or another, including freedom of being their own boss ('You just swap one boss for 10!', acknowledged one freelance editor), money, variety of work, family responsibilities, flexible hours, geographic reasons, a dislike of commuting. Freelance editors often work from the SOHO (Small Office Home Office) at either a Mac or PC, with a telephone, modem and fax to ensure that even if the

employer is a Sydney-based publisher and your author is in
Perth, the freelancer can work from Adelaide with minimal
problems. Although New Zealand is smaller, the same difficulties with distance can be overcome.

Types of editors

Acquisitions or commissioning

Acquisition (commissioning) editors commission (or acquire)
titles or ranges of titles on behalf of their publishing house.
In a small publishing house, they may undertake all the roles
of a publisher, or in a larger house, they may only acquire
books for a specific area and, with a number of other
commissioning editors, report to the publisher. An acquisitions editor will have to have a good understanding of
marketing and an eye for trends in their area. They may
monitor particular markets for forthcoming trends and fads,
identify new opportunities and keep up to date with the
international, as well as the national publishing scene. Along
with keeping in touch with leading authors and experts in
their field who may be potential authors, they will negotiate
contracts, assess potential for new titles and reprints,
manage multiple author projects, budgets and supervise a
range of in-house and freelance editorial staff. As well as
this, they may also work with favoured or important
authors on their manuscripts, retaining a hands-on
approach. The direction of the design brief also comes from
the commissioning editor, as does input on the layout and
production.

Along with the publisher, the acquisitions editor may also
set the tone of the publishing house not only through the
type of works they bring in, but by producing the style
guide. Each publishing house will have its own style guide
(a 'how-to' manual) which gives information for authors
and freelance editors. These booklets are passed on to
authors at the time of signing the contract and are meant
as a reference tool for the author to use. They also save
unnecessary repeat communication between author and
editor and publisher. The style guide will contain some
mixture of the following information:

- history or background of the publishing house, including information about the types of books published
- author's responsibilities
- basic publishing process information
- presentation of the manuscript from the author to the publisher
- grammar preferences—for example, some publishers spell all numbers under ten, then use figures after that. Or the guide will establish the points to follow to ensure a consistent style for capitalisation and numbering or use of symbols
- advice on tables, indexes and bibliographies is also given.

Structural

Structural editors are senior editors who deal with the structure of the text. They look at the book as a whole, although they may also undertake the copy editing as well. They suggest changes that will allow the manuscript to flow more smoothly and make more sense. They suggest alterations to sentences, substitute or delete words that are repeated, untangle passages where the meaning is unclear, and on the macro level advise changes to the chapter sequence. They will often radically reshape a book—for example, reducing a 230,000 word manuscript to 150,000 words, or a 15,000 word text to 10,000 words.

Copy

'To succeed as a copy editor you require an excellent eye for detail, possess good, clear handwriting and have a determination to go over the same text again and again until you are satisfied with the result.'
Freelance Copy editor

Copy editors are dealing with the day-to-day nitty gritty of spelling and grammar. Where do the prepositions fall? Do we follow the American spelling because the author is from New York, or the Australian because it is being published over here? They battle with authors over matters of grammar ('I had one author who scattered commas through a manuscript like tadpoles in a pond,' was a comment overheard at a Society of Editors function). Copy editors may work solely on updating new editions of travel or text or reference works. They may undertake whole books or single chapters, depending on their speciality.

Indexers

Indexing is a specialist field within the editorial process. Many editors will never handle an index: either they do not work on titles that require its inclusion, or the work is fielded out to an indexing specialist. Most serious non-fiction titles and many general non-fiction titles will require an index that is appropriate both to the reader's needs and expectations. Generally the cost of an index is borne by the author, although for an in-house title (one that is produced in-house either as a new publication or one that may be an amalgam of several titles, as often happens in the case of cookbooks, for instance) that may not have an individual author, then the cost obviously will be carried by the publisher.

Indexers always like to be contacted and consulted as early as possible regarding a new book, in order to determine the index requirements. Editors normally will prefer to work with an indexer who has experience on similar titles. Issues that the editor and indexer may discuss include scheduling (when the editor requires the index to be completed and delivered), format (whether the index is to be submitted on disk and as hard copy), the computer to be used (PC or Mac), which software format (such as, Index 4, Cindex, Macrex), the page layout (1, 2 or 3 columns, font and point size), the maximum number of pages available, and whether the indexer is required to proofread the index once it has been typeset.

To give you an insider's viewpoint, here are two first-hand accounts from experienced indexers:

> *The indexer's quote typically comes out between $700 and $2500, though the printout is hardly bulky and the typeset version runs to only a few pages in length. Does this really represent value for money? Publishers might well decide that an indexer is a luxury, that the author can compile the index cost-free—instantly boosting the profit margin. Authors often agree because they know that otherwise the indexing cost will likely be debited against their already*

modest royalties. But if author and indexer each set about the same task independently, would there be any real difference in their outcomes?

Sometimes no, but far more often yes. The answer depends on the author's feel for the task and on the complexity of the index required. In general, the more intricately layered and cross-referenced the end product needs to be, and the more inexperienced the author is at the task, the more vital it is to have an indexer. Let there be no doubt: indexing is highly demanding: it requires an ability to think structurally, involves seemingly endless hours of methodical work and intense concentration. You emerge from it as if from a non-stop interrogation lasting anywhere from three days to three weeks, totally drained. It is a task for either the blissfully ignorant or the masochistic.

Many professional indexers work full-time and often specialise in subjects on which they have particular expertise. In this way, they might deal exclusively with books on Australian history, or natural science, or business management. Others might be part-time or occasional indexers, spending the rest of their time cataloguing, editing or otherwise bringing chaos to order. For all of us an easy indexing project is one involving mainly proper nouns— names of things, people and places where there are no alternative forms. But let it be a bulky illustrated tome filled with complicated concepts that reader–researchers will need to be able to locate speedily, written by an author with an engagingly discursive narrative but a loose concept of 'the big picture' and the way constituent parts mesh together, or written by numerous contributors who seem to have little in common methodologically or stylistically, and you are in for an battle. Especially if last-minute repaging widely affects page turnovers.

As a full-time editor, I index infrequently. I really enjoy the mental challenge of indexing—especially with the complex jobs—but always feel burned out afterwards. Even extensive structural editing seems easy in comparison. As an indexer I warmed up on a short, single-issue history (the publisher courageously but quite characteristically

expressed his total confidence—and gave me three whole days to complete the task), then moved straight along into a massive anthropological study where each of the place names had a non-English alternative to be cross-referenced, where the several hundred personal names all had up to three different standard forms plus various diminutives used interchangeably, and where the general items included many dozens of clans, sub-clans and other complicated layerings. After that, I felt that I could tackle anything (though I insist on indexing books I have edited myself—a quirky measure which gives me thorough knowledge of the subject at hand and of the way the book has been constructed). And I gained the greatest respect for full-time indexers. In sum, any committed indexer is worth at least every dollar they charge. But this will hardly be news to any author who has ever attempted to complete the task themselves, or to any reader–researcher who has ever searched in vain through a badly constructed index for information which should be accessible without an entire re-read.
Diane Carlyle, Freelance Indexer and Editor

Most people getting in to indexing usually come to it from either a librarianship or editing background, however this is not essential. Providing you have a good knowledge of your subject field, have an analytical mind, and an eye for detail you have the makings of an indexer.
Max McMaster, Master Indexing

The vision

Working on books you love, authors hovering full of gratitude for your suggestions to alter their manuscript from something disorganised to a thing of beauty, invitations to literary festivals fill the in-tray as do fascinating, well-crafted manuscripts by highly esteemed authors able to spell and write with clarity. There is plenty of time to discuss the latest award-winning novel with like-minded colleagues and peruse the new edition of *Australian Book Review*, *NZ Books* and the *Times Literary Supplement*.

The reality

Working on several books at the one time, touchy authors

who resist changing even a comma and hate the cover ideas, deadlines looming, freelance editors taking longer than promised. Marketing wants the manuscript corrected so they can send out proofs to encourage extracts in magazines, the index is incomplete and another author cannot complete the latest revisions for tomorrow, as she's in labour/he's attending his mother's funeral.

My life as an editor

Here is a brief summary of the sort of tasks an editor will encounter in the course of their work:

'I'm a non-fiction editor working on HarperCollins trade list. I work from the Melbourne office (our head office is in Sydney) and the list includes books on biography, health and parenting issues, popular psychology and spirituality, and even (occasionally) fiction in the New-Age type fiction. The sort of responsibilities I have include overseeing a project from manuscript stage to finally becoming a book, editing manuscripts (both copy editing and structural editing), proofreading, writing briefs for the cover and internal design, writing back cover copy, liaising with authors and indexers and loads of administrative work!'

Carolyn Leslie, Editor, Non-fiction, HarperCollins

How I became an editor . . .

Susan Keogh is a senior editor at Melbourne University Press, Past President of the Society of Editors (Vic) and has a BA Hons. Susan is currently studying at the University of Melbourne for a Graduate Diploma in Media, Information Technology and Communications Law, and is responsible for all the science titles published at Melbourne University Press. Susan is 30 years of age. Here she tells how she became an editor:

In 1985, toward the end of the second year of my degree at the University of Melbourne, I saw a notice in the student employment office, 'Wanted strong student to move books into the new warehouse at Melbourne University Press'. 'Ah, books, publishing—that's something I could do,' I thought. I rang and spoke to the secretary to the Director. She obviously wanted a male or someone with plenty of

*muscle, as she was not overly enthusiastic about my appli-
cation. However, I persevered and she eventually gave in. I
then spent three days moving hundreds of boxes of books
such as the* Atlas of Australian Birds *in the company of a
couple of very strong off-duty policemen (just as well that
they had muscles!). Some time after that, I saw an advertisement in the* Age *for the University Bookroom, wanting
experienced sales staff to operate the cash registers over the
summer. Although I didn't have any sales experience, I went
in, obtained an interview with Bruce, the manager, and
when asked for experience, said, 'I have worked for your
trade division'. Bruce said, 'Hmm . . . ' and so I spent the
next two weeks in their basement, pricing remainder stock.
One thing led to another, and I worked on a casual basis
in the bookshop from then on, for the next two years—
pricing, sales, stocking the shelves and administrative work.*

*In August of my final year, my mother noticed another
advertisement in the* Age *employment section under 'Publishing Opportunity'. Basically, MUP wanted a
receptionist/typist. I applied, passed the typing test and they
kindly waited for me to graduate. At the end of 1987, I
handed in my last essay, took a week off to get organised
and buy some clothes other than jeans, then started in
November.*

*I spent 14 months working on reception—I opened all
the mail, typed up editorial and production correspondence
and reports for the accountant. It was a good way not only
to see which titles were selling, but also to gain a valuable
overview of the publishing company, as I could see how all
the different departments interacted with each other. During
this time, while I was pleased for the chance to work in a
publishing house, I felt that editing was my career, so I also
edited two and a half titles under the guidance of the
Editorial Manager, while still working in this administrative
role. Just after the then Director Peter Ryan retired, I said
to my supervisors, 'You advertised this position as a publishing opportunity, I'd like to take on the opportunity or
else I will have to start looking elsewhere'. When the new
Director started, it was put to him that I be promoted to
full-time Editorial Assistant and that we get another recep-*

tionist. He agreed, and it was no more mail, no more telephones! I started under Wendy Sutherland, who was then MUP's Editorial Manager and who has now gone freelance. Invariably she would point out something to me that I had missed, but working with her was great as I was learning something new. I'm not sure if the reality of publishing matched the fantasy, because I was not really sure that I had a fantasy of what it would be like, although I did think that I would start at MUP, then move on, but MUP keeps reinventing itself and now I have been at MUP for nearly ten years! The Director sets the tone of the house and gives a different feel to the place, and since I have been here we have had four changes of director.

What titles do I like the most? I always enjoy most the book on which I am currently working. If you don't like the books you are working on, then no-one else in the publishing house will, and the project will die.

I'm now the editor responsible for scientific titles, which is an area of publishing that I never contemplated before I joined MUP, as I wanted to work on 'literature'. In Australia, we have a number of the world's best scientists, such as the best beetle scientist and leading astrophotographers—it is quite a buzz working on titles with people who are the best in their field. One title I edited, The Insects of Australia, won both an APA design award and the 1992 Whitley Medal for the best book on natural history of Australian animals. This title I found to be quite exciting, and I spent roughly a year working on it, and I was really pleased with the result. When I started, MUP had just got a computer system for the accounts and the inventory. No-one else had a computer, not even a word processor! Now we have launched our own home page on the World Wide Web, and it has been interesting to see the changes coming through. Now all our design and typesetting are done on the desktop, but often the nature of the book I am working on requires that I edit hard copy.

You have to like authors and be able to communicate and get along with people to be a successful editor. You must also have an obsessive personality, ability to touch type, and clear handwriting! I first got into publishing

*because I liked books, but I have stayed in publishing
because I like authors.*

Salaries/Rates of pay

The following are the Australian Book Industry Award 1997
rates of pay for editors:

Level	Weekly		Annual	
Level 1 (Trainee)				
Upon commencement	$441.20	(463.30)	22,942.40	(24,091.60)
After six months	482.90	(507.00)	25,110.80	(26,364.00)
Level 2 (Book Editor)				
Grade 1	524.60	(550.80)	27,279.20	(28,641.60)
Grade 2	545.50	(572.80)	28,366.00	(29,785.60)
Grade 3	587.20	(616.60)	30,534.40	(32,063.20)
Grade 4	628.90	(660.30)	32,702.80	(34,335.60)
Level 3 (Senior Editor)				
Grade 1	670.70	(704.20)	34,876.40	(36,618.40)
Grade 2	712.40	(748.00)	37,044.80	(38,896.00)
Grade 3	816.70	(857.50)	42,468.40	(44,590.00)

(Figures in brackets are the VDU allowance, payable to editors
working on-screen.)

For further information contact the Media, Entertainment
and Arts Alliance (MEAA) in Australia on (02) 9279 0500.

Editing courses and education

In these days of increasing professionalism, specialisation
and competition, it is becoming more important to get
proper accreditation. There are a plethora of editing courses
emerging (see Chapter 11 'Courses available' for more information). Here are some comments from editors about the
advantages of doing a course of study in this area:

'The best course I ever did was the editing course run by the
Society of Editors. It was time-efficient and covered the
mechanics of editing—learning the editorial and proofreading
marks, discussing the responsibilities and boundaries of being
an editor and even suggestions on how to look for work!'
Carolyn Leslie, Editor, Non-fiction, HarperCollins

'Check the course outline carefully before you embark on it,

to make sure that it's going to take you in the direction you want. Gain as much from a course as you can. There's no point in going to a course that has stated its content as being discussion of, say, issues in electronic publishing, and then feeling disappointed because you thought it would cover training in the use of a specific software program. Read the course content before you sign up! The Macquarie (NSW) and RMIT (Vic) courses both provide good all-round grounding in publishing. Some editorial courses are very specific and are excellent for editors and would-be editors. Lots of software companies are currently advertising "seminars" which often turn out to be merely glorified product launches.'
Penny Martin, Senior Publishing Consultant, Harcourt Brace & Co.

'"The Introduction to Book Publishing" course at MLC was a good starting point which teaches the basics. For the finer points, the "Graduate Diploma in Editing and Publishing" at RMIT has made my learning go through the roof! This course has been invaluable in helping me with the day-to-day aspects of my job.'
Kristen Baragwanath, Acquisitions Editor, Schools Division, McGraw-Hill

'Undertaking a publishing course helped me to decide where my interests in the book trade lay.'
Michelle Phillips, Publishing Assistant, ACER

'I found that doing an introductory publishing course was a good way to help me decide if I would make a change from Law to Publishing. I then undertook the Monash Graduate Diploma of Publishing and found it very useful to consolidate my choice of editing as a career.'
Michelle Atkins, Primary Editor/Copyright & Permissions Editor/Contracts Controller, Nelson ITP

Professional groups

The groups that will serve your needs and keep you informed as an editor are the Society of Editors (state-based), Australian Society of Indexers, Galley Club (state-based), and Women in Publishing (NSW and WA).

Conclusion

There is a wide variety of positions within the editing field.

In order to succeed in your aim to become an editor, you must consider the following:

- Persevere, since it may take some time to achieve your 'ideal' position.
- Undertake a respected editorial course at a tertiary or TAFE institution.
- Join the Society of Editors in your state, attend their meetings and their own training courses.
- Consider undertaking work experience in a book or magazine publishing house, or at a printing company in order to gain valuable on-the-job exposure.
- Ensure that you are realistic in your expectations.

4 Marketing as a career

'I got a job with a direct marketing firm called IBIS, who dealt with a lot of publishers. This was a brilliant place to start, direct marketing was then in its infancy and now it's become a really key area — you need to know about direct marketing to do almost anything, really. This was also an excellent place from which to be thinking about a job in publishing. I was dealing with lots of different publishers, selling them IBIS's services, and I got to see a lot of different standards and styles in publishing and think very clearly about where I wanted to end up.'
Alison Baverstock, UK Freelance Marketing Consultant and Author of How to Market Books

'Working in marketing means that I am exposed to a really broad view of what my publishing company is about.'
Marketing Assistant

'When people (outside publishing) find out that I work in the marketing department of a publisher, they assume that I do things like arranging publicity for books — they don't realise that there is more to marketing, such as strategic and financial planning and forecasting.'
Marketing Administrator

'Everything that affects our customers — for example, sales, publicity, logistics, customer service — comes under marketing.'
Bookshop Marketing Coordinator

41

'As a marketing assistant, my work is primarily in the publicity area — the most satisfying thing is seeing a favourable review appear — particularly if it's big and has an illustration!'
Melinda Bufton, Marketing Assistant, Alison Aprhys Marketing & Promotions

Definition

Marketing is made up of three components: sales volume, customer focus and coordinated effort. Without these three items in balance, the marketing of a title, imprint, range or publishing house will be out of sorts and ineffective. In a broader application, marketing encompasses a wide variety of areas including publicity, public relations, promotions, sales, customer service and market research, publicity, and in some publishing houses the sales department as well. Although sales is definitely a part of the marketing mix, in this book I am dealing with sales careers in publishing and bookselling in separate chapters. This is because many publishers have a separate sales division, although the sales representatives may report to the marketing manager or director. The jobs in sales and marketing within a publishing house are vastly different to the job of a bookseller.

The marketing manager may oversee a publicity tour for a visiting author, arrange for an extract of a new title to appear in a magazine or newspaper, arrange for advertising to appear in a trade journal, oversee staff putting together the new release information sheets for the sales representatives, approve the point of sale material for a new book, comment on new proposed book cover designs, collate and market research data, and keep up to date with marketing trends in Australia and internationally. Marketing means different things to different publishing houses. There may be a marketing staff of ten or a staff of two. That staff may work on trade, technical, business, educational book or non-book products such as CD-ROM, audio books or books on disk. Certainly marketing used to be an area you could enter via the sales department; these days a recognised qualification is increasingly important. It is no longer enough to understand sales and sales alone. Strategic planning, long-range market research and forecasting now play a bigger part in the marketing manager's job. Books take some time to produce, so the need to ensure that the publisher is not producing books out of sync with reading trends is very important. Many marketing departments are broken down into several areas, such as publicity, promotions, sales and general marketing.

The vision

Your department is well organised and efficient, all deadlines are met. The CEO sends you a memo saying how pleased the board are with your strategic marketing plan for the next financial year and inviting you to go to several international book fairs. All your authors are charming, polite, meet their schedules and call to thank you for arranging such favourable publicity. The literary editors of newspapers, magazines and specialist journals are clamouring for review copies and interviews. Your sales force have surpassed projected sales figures and there are minimal returns. Booksellers vote your company 'Publisher of the Year'.

The reality

Deadlines are running amok; the printers have rung to say they'll be late with your new brochures; the newspaper has lost your advertisement copy; book reviews appear months before (or months after) the author tour; the author gets pneumonia in Switzerland a week before the launches in Sydney and Auckland; the literary editor of a major publication has not received the couriered copy of the manuscript; the financial controller fights you for budget share in the department meeting; the publisher won't budge on a cover that your sales force hate and insist won't sell, the production manager informs you that the book for which you have organised a national publicity and advertising campaign will be late and miss the deadline; and reviews appearing for the new blockbuster your publishing house has just released are terrible.

Publicity

Publicity is unpaid advertising. Publicity covers items from author interviews on air to book reviews in the newspaper, from individual title publicity to putting the corporate point of view across as required. A publicist may work on one or many tasks at a time. When undertaking book publicity, she or he may have lots of titles on the go at once, however they will all be at different stages of the publicity process. One title may be at the review send-out stage, another title will have media clamouring for interviews or extracts, a third title's publicity may just be commencing to appear, while a fourth will be at the end of the publicity cycle. Although 'free' in terms of placement costs compared to advertising, publicity still incurs costs such as postage, couriers, printing, telephone and fax calls. Some publicists think there is no such thing as bad publicity, while others are more circumspect.

In the course of a single day a publicist may undertake the following array of tasks:

- creating, maintaining and updating of media databases
- creating and forwarding releases, review copies and media packs to the appropriate media
- coaching authors to speak with media or appear on media (giving them tips to help them relax or give a better interview — for example, asking them not to swivel in their chair during an in-studio radio interview as their voice will swing in and out of range in front of the microphone)
- producing catalogues and brochures for sales representatives and direct mail programs
- arranging an author tour: handling travel and accommodation bookings, liaising with media for author tours and interviews, scheduling in attendances at bookshops, writers' festivals, special interest group meetings
- organising a book launch: obtaining someone suitable to launch the title, guest list, invitations and RSVP, venue, catering, media liaison before, during and after the launch, and book sales at the event
- managing customer liaison to ensure that the retailers and booksellers know when the publicity for a given title will 'hit', so they can be prepared and order copies of the book.

My work in publicity means . . .

To put you more in the picture, here are comments from a few experienced publicists:

'Basically, I allocate, formulate and direct all advertising and publicity for HarperCollins' range of books, including author tours and extracts. I formulate and manage the marketing budget and allocate the publicity resources to best promote our titles. One of my foremost responsibilities is to liaise with media and authors for the best possible media.'
Christine Farmer, National Publicity Manager, HarperCollins

'Being a publicist means being able to juggle ten things at once; update the mailing lists, book the launch venue, calm down your author, chat up the media and keep your cool with the fax machine going berserk.'
Anonymous Publicist

Skills required to succeed in publicity

If you think publicity is for you, just check that you have the following:
- Persistence — 'Sometimes you have to work really hard at getting through to the media, but you can't give up after just one try.'
- Communications — 'You have to be able to effectively communicate with a wide variety of people: media, authors, sales staff, booksellers, reviewer and publishing staff. As well as an excellent phone manner, good listening skills are paramount.'
- Organisation — 'With so much happening in my department, if someone is not organised, they won't stay here long — we often have 20 or 30 titles happening at any one time and we can't afford to have disorganised staff.'
- Enthusiasm — 'Often the books you are publicising have no personal appeal to you, but you have to remember that they will appeal to some media and some customers, so you must be as enthusiastic as possible in order to do your job.'
- Stamina — 'Author tours are either heaven or hell! You have to be able to cope with everything at once and you

are often a combination of author's best friend, psychiatrist, minder and gofer.'

• Personality — 'A good publicist has a good personality. It's important that they be able to relate to media and authors.'

Marketing manager/director

The marketing manager or director is responsible for the staff in their department. They oversee everything from budgets to catalogues. They may do less hands-on work than their subordinates, instead they are looking at the strategic planning of their division and the publishing company or bookshop as a whole.

Two directors outline their responsibilities:

'My responsibility covers the consumer division sales, profits, marketing and staff. Also I set strategies to achieve these goals.'
Mary Howell, Sales & Marketing Director, Hodder Headline

'As I'm responsible for the sales and marketing side of the business, this covers everything from sales training, sales targets, merchandising, in-store promotions, customer loyalty programs, direct marketing and catalogue and database management.'
Caroline Radford, Managing Director, Sales & Marketing, The Technical Book & Magazine Company

Promotions

Promotions have a definite commencement and completion date. They can range from promoting an imprint, a single title or a range of publisher's or author's books. Generally, promotions require the support of booksellers to have 'legs', otherwise they will not work. Therefore, it is up to the promotions coordinator to create and manage promotions with which the booksellers will become involved, thus passing on their enthusiasm to their customers. Like other aspects of marketing, they require efficient organisation and management.

'Promoting an imprint is similar to promoting a particular book or author — you have to know your market and how best to reach it. I get ideas from all over the place, not just

from the competition, but from the Internet, media, sports, and often retailers have great ideas that I can adapt for our use.'
Promotions Consultant

Market research

Market research involves finding out what the market really wants, which trends are merely fads and which trends are leading somewhere, what opportunities are there for a publisher to bring out new titles or to reprint older ones. For example, the BBC series of Jane Austen's *Pride and Prejudice* dramatically increased sales and awareness of all of that author's titles, as well as generating interest in similar titles by authors such as the Brontë sisters and George Eliot. This fascination with British period fiction led publishers to look more closely at their older titles for opportunities that would dovetail with this trend.

Booksellers and sales representatives are obvious choices for information regarding reading trends. Booksellers, because they have the job of actually selling the books to the readers, have a very good knowledge of what their particular customers want. Some specialist booksellers act as readers for publishers advising on how well they feel the book will sell, thereby suggesting the size of the print run.

Quite often, if an author approaches a publisher with a publishing proposal, the publisher will request that the author prove to them that there is a market for their particular title. With non-fiction, many publishers use outside readers to gauge the quality and viability of the work. For example, if you are a science editor for an academic publishing house, whilst you may feel comfortable editing titles from physics to astronomy to botany, you are not likely to be an expert in all these fields, so you will contact a specialist and pass the manuscript on to him or her for their professional assessment.

'We are often approached by small or self-publishers who want to know if there is a viable market for a title. What they really want to know is if they publish a particular title, will they make a profit.'
Marketing Consultant

Marketing qualifications

What sort of qualifications do workers in this area have and find useful?

'I've undertaken a Public Relations course at University of Technology, an Advertising/Script writing course at Sydney Technical College and a Marketing course at Macquarie University. Currently I'm enrolled for a marketing management course.'
Christine Farmer, National Publicity Manager, HarperCollins

'In order, my qualifications are a Diploma of Teaching, Bachelor of Education, Graduate Diploma in Librarianship and I'll complete a Master of Business (Marketing) in May 1998.'
Patricia Genat, Head of Division, ACER

'"Finance for non-financial people" and lots and lots of specialist industry courses.'
Mary Howell, Sales & Marketing Director, Hodder Headline

'Bachelor of Business — Marketing.'
Carolyn Radford, Managing Director, Sales & Marketing,
Technical Book & Magazine Company

'I started off with a Bachelor of Business Marketing and I'm halfway through a Masters in Marketing. At this level, the number crunching and the management skills become so much more important. It's crucial to stay on top of these issues.'
Marketing Manager

'I'm studying a part-time post-graduate marketing course. While it's tiring balancing a family with work and study, I have found it very useful as I am able to make practical use of the theoretical knowledge.'
Marketing Manager

'It was only by attending an APA course on marketing that I realised that this was what really attracted me — not production or editing which was all I had considered up till then.'
Promotions Assistant

These days a tertiary qualification is a must. Generally, it is less important to know at which institution someone has studied their marketing course, than the fact that they actually have done study at the tertiary level. Of course, if you are going to put in the time, effort (and the money) to attend, you want to make sure that the course you attend is accredited and recognised by state/national educational bodies, such as the State Training Board. By attending a formal marketing course, you will be exposed to new ideas and be able to learn marketing theory. While these theories are constantly being updated, the foundations behind them are solid and will give you foundations to build on when you are creating or updating marketing programs for your company.

Complement your university or TAFE study with industry courses such as those run by the ABA, APA and Galley Club and in New Zealand by Booksellers New Zealand and the Book Publishers Association. Marketing is a dynamic industry and it is crucial that you stay up to date with new trends, ideas and theories. You need to constantly be in touch with new ideas inside and outside of the book trade. Don't ever assume that you know all about it — as our customers change, marketing must constantly evolve too.

5 Production as a career

'I decided publishing would be nice; applied for the first job I saw in the paper to do with publishing (for a production assistant) and got the job!'
Sally Stokes, Production Manager, Lansdowne Publishing/Macquarie Dictionary

'As a design and production assistant, I work in the design department assisting the designers with the preparation of pre-press material. A typical day for me includes putting files on cartridge zip, doing low resolution scans, photocopying and relief reception work.'
Paula Barrios, Production Assistant, Reed Education

'A typical day for me? It depends on the day! I can plan to complete a couple of key tasks and then about seven different things get lobbed in from left field and I end up having checked a proof or two, briefed an editor, negotiated with an author, dealt with a book design one way or the other, devised a budget and/or schedule for a new idea, dealt with staffing issues and maybe management budgets as well. Until recently I was also teaching at Macquarie University, so some days ended up with classes too.'
Penny Martin, Senior Publishing Consultant, Harcourt Brace & Co.

'I started out with a BA degree, diploma in journalism and diploma in secondary teacher training. I gained work experience in newspaper reporting, magazine editing, journal editing,

marketing, government publishing, independent publishing, and ultimately set up my own publishing business which runs: a publishing service to government and corporates; a publishing training course (and literary publishing imprint); and Lincoln University Press (an academic publishing imprint).'
Daphne Brasell, Publishing Director, Daphne Brasell Associates Ltd, Wellington, New Zealand

'I am responsible for the cost, scheduling and quality controls of all MUP products — printed and electronic — and have staff responsibility for everybody in the editorial and production departments.'
Andrew Watson, Assistant Director, Melbourne University Press

Definition

People often think of editorial as the key factor in publishing, unaware of the many other steps that a manuscript must go through, complicated and crucial stages, in order to reach the point of becoming a book ready for the sales representative to sell in to the bookseller. These steps following the editorial stage are called production.

The production process

The production process commences once the more intangible aspects of the book have been decided, such as, the readership or market and how the book will be promoted. The production process has to do with such tangible aspects as the size of the print run, the price, date of publication, format, budget, quality, design, layout, illustrations, paper stock, binding, and the printing method to be used.

Production manager

The Production Controller is responsible for part of a list, while the Production Manager is responsible for a whole department. In a large company, a Production Director will be responsible for several departments, such as trade and education.

The production controller or manager manages the production team and is responsible for the scheduling and costing of the books being produced.

The production department in a publishing house may

be comprised of in-house or freelance staff in the following positions: designers, printers, illustrators, typesetters, DTP and administrative assistants as required. Obviously many of these freelance or in-house staff are specialists in one area or another; for example, a designer may specialise in working with illustrated or academic titles; a typesetter may work exclusively with law texts or fiction; some illustrators only work in a particular medium such as pen and ink, water colours or pencil.

The production staff must have good contacts with a wide range of freelancers or contract workers. Freelance staff may be booked well in advance (especially when working on a series or a long project), so it is important for the production manager to be able to allocate work according to the need and availability. This allows the publisher to engage a designer to work on an imprint or title according to schedule and within budget as required.

Generally the production manager or controller will brief the illustrator, designer and other staff as required to ensure that there is complete understanding of the job. Ensuring that the involved parties meet allows the discussion and avoidance of potential problems, and the various people can see what their contribution will be to the bigger picture. The production manager knows that, while each member of the team brings skills, experience and ability, it is up to the manager to ensure that the end result emerges as envisaged.

The vision

All your books win APA design awards or the Montana awards, there is never any problem with the artwork, your printers are devoted to your books, all the authors (hence the editorial team) run to schedule. Paper prices are on a downward cost spin. Printers are looking for work and are offering good print quality, low prices and promise to meet deadlines. Your artists and designers have a wonderful insight into your instructions and actually follow them. The sales team love the covers you present, the booksellers think they are beautiful to look at and a real selling point, and the customers adore the look and feel of your books.

The reality

Your professional life is ruled by the clock due to costs and the demands of the budget. Much of your printing is done off-shore, so you have to be absolutely on top of all your schedules. Your typesetters and DTP are often wanting to produce something that is more aesthetic, but the sales manager insists they will not be liked by the booksellers. The authors are at loggerheads with your design/production of 'their books' and sulk when the editor or you point out the relevant clauses in the contract to them. It goes without saying that your favourite freelance designer/typesetter/illustrator goes to Bali, the Bay of Islands or has a baby just when you most need them.

'Production people are a special breed. They must be pragmatic as they need to be able to deal with a variety of important tasks at the same time — not everyone can cope with this. For example, in a typically hectic day you may be dealing with authors, printers, designers and other in-house staff, speaking on two phones at the same time. And in whatever they do, they need to keep an eye on the costs, schedules and quality. Production people straddle the huge gulf between the concept and the finished product.'
Andrew Watson, Assistant Director, Melbourne University Press

The typesetter

Traditionally, many typesetters have come from the printing trade, however, increasingly typesetters are emerging from the area of DTP, backed up with solid industry courses. The typesetter or image-maker is in an area that has revolutionised the way books are published. It is a dynamic, fast-paced world, where today's technology will be obsolete within a very short time. Desktop computers are offering an increasingly sophisticated method of producing type onto paper or film.

'The way I got into publishing was by mistake and I loved it from the start! I applied for a job as a hand compositor (hand setting type) and became an apprentice printer. During my first year, I saw the way the industry was progressing away from hot metal and cold comp, toward computers. So I enrolled at what was then the Printer's College in North Melbourne (now

a part of RMIT) in a Certificate of Advanced Printing, so that I would be keeping up to date with the coming technology. Currently I am the manager at Southbank Book which means that I'm responsible for the successful production of books on behalf of our clients, the publishers. As well as that, I manage marketing and sales, overall financial matters and the staff for my division.'
Michael Holman, Manager, Southbank Book

The illustrator

The illustrator must interpret the text in accordance with the wishes of the author and the editor. The illustration — be it a photomontage, pastel, line drawing or pen and ink — must match the book's mood. The illustrations must be appropriate to the content, the text, the binding, the paper — it requires a holistic approach.

'On one children's book we had, it was apparent that the illustrator had not read the book, because one very important map sequence was illustrated with the journey in the wrong order. And every kid who read the book would point this out.'
Marketing Manager

The designer

'I like being a book designer, partly because of my client Random House — they are easy to work with, offer me scope, and a wide variety of work. It's not always pushing the interest of the corporate world, it allows me to work at home which suits me as I have a small child. Out of all the areas of graphic design, books are the most fascinating.'
Yolande Gray, Freelance Book Designer, Winner of the Joyce Nicholson Award for best designed book and Australian Paper Award for the best designed book over $50

'With one recent book one of the editors, an acquaintance of Michael Leunig, asked Leunig to design the cover. The cover design was immediately identifiable, simple and very appealing. I'm confident that the cover certainly contributed to the very healthy sales we achieved.'
Helen Celerier, Medical Marketing Manager, Blackwell Science Asia

'We have some designers who will do both because the cover of a book needs to reflect the style of typography inside of the

book. We've got one book, for example, where the typography and the look of the cover is very different from the typography used for headings and layout on the inside. Both are fantastic but they just don't match each other and to me it's a bit disconcerting to see that. So there needs to be some kind of coordination and cohesion between the text designer and the cover designer. There are some designers who just take one look at the title and dream something up with their first instinct. I instruct the designers that they do need to read these design briefs. They are very important because our publisher and our marketing people know what is required.'
Gabby Luhede, Production Controller, Melbourne University Press

'The main thing about deciding upon a book design is to think about who the audience is, who is the book going to appeal to, and what kind of people are in the target market. The best result comes when the designer takes a close interest in the whole project, including reading the book. Editors are not always visually literate, and it's fantastic when the designer picks up on what is said and produces a cover that contains the essence of what the author and publisher wish to communicate to the audience. It's a real team effort.'
Erica Irving, Associate Publisher, Books for Children and Young Adults, Penguin Books Australia

'When you are producing a title on an annual basis, you want it to look good, you don't want to radically alter the design from the previous editions, but you also want the customer to know when they look at it, that they recognise that it's the new or latest edition. Once or twice I've been in bookshops and overheard people discussing the cover of a book, and I'm always really interested to hear what they say. So far it's always been favourable!'
Leon Kowalski, Research/Editorial Assistant, Penguin Books Australia

'Over time [at McPhee Gribble] I learnt about the whole spectrum of publishing. In this position I felt involved with the whole process, authors were always in and out, we were aware of all the marketing and publishing decisions that were made. This was one of the brilliant things about the company: you felt that you were involved with the whole publishing process. A big part of the success of any design is how well the publisher briefs the designer. It makes a huge difference! It also means that a certain level of trust is involved. Now that I have proven myself, the publisher giving me the brief will often leave me to work out the vision and a look that suits the title. I like to be involved in the whole process, not just making a "pretty cover".'

Mary Callaghan, Book Designer of The Orchard *by Drusilla Modjeska,* The Riders *by Tim Winton,* A Recipe for Dreaming *by Bryce Courtenay*

'Usually I'm contacted quite early in the piece, sometimes the author has contacted me even before they go to a publisher. This is good because it means that I've been recommended! I expect to be given the manuscript, the pictures (I almost always work on books with lots of illustrations), as well as technical details such as size, probable paper to be used and printing production level from the production manager.'

Alison Forbes, Book Designer of The Art of the First Fleet *and* Vital Connections

'I think it's really important with book covers to look to booksellers. They're seeing every day what people are drawn to, what they are pulling off the shelves. I worked as a bookseller for a little while and it was a fabulous background for marketing, as you see on a day-to-day basis what book designs work, and what book designs are not effective.'

Emma Hollister, Marketing Co-ordinator, Melbourne University Press

'Book design, like any other design form, is about integrating and rationalising the elements so that the result appears simple and direct and the integrity of the book's purpose remains intact.'

Zoe Murphy, Freelance Book Designer, Winner of Weldon Hardy Young Designer's Award

Designers are responsible for the overall look and feel of the book. They look after the layout, cover or jacket, paper type, typeface used, illustration or photograph placement, colour and, of course, design. Design is an important element of a title as it will be a definite method of attracting interest and sales. Whether it is an arresting cover design, the layout of the illustrations or photographs, or the look of the text on the pages, design plays an important part of

making the book attractive to the market. This is high-
lighted by the Australian Publishers Association who have
every year since 1953, presented the Design Awards. These
awards are for outstanding books in various categories such
as Illustrated Books, Primary Education, Secondary Education, Multi-media and Paperback. In New Zealand there's
the Montana Awards as well as the GP Print Book Design
Awards, begun in 1997. These awards are highly coveted
and are extremely competitive. Designers tend to have completed a tertiary course specialising in their medium of
applied art, and then honed their skills on the job. Designers
can work on a wide range of titles or focus on their
specialisation.

Visual planning is the focus of the book designer. The
designer must work within the time frame, budget and
technical constraints to produce an image that is aestheti-
cally pleasing, while remaining attuned to the target market.
The designer must also take into account the views of the
editor, as well as input from the production, sales and
marketing departments.

Like their customers, booksellers can respond very
strongly to designs:

'When the Penguin reps first showed us Elizabeth Jolley's
Orchard Thieves, we all stood around and stroked the cover.
I think it was the first of the new matt covers I had seen.'
Melbourne Bookseller

'When I first saw *New Food*, it was like WOW! The purple
background with the yellow pear! We all loved it and (more
importantly!) so did our customers!'
Melbourne Bookseller

'Robert Dessaix's *Night Letters* is such a beautiful book . . .
it is still selling strongly — I think while many people love the
writing, the look of this title is very strong.'
Sydney Bookseller

'*Zoo* is the book that I most admire. Strong graphics, great
photos — especially the elephant on the cover — we put some
in the window and the customers would come in and demand
to see it!'
Country Bookseller

'As soon as we picked up Stephanie Alexander's cookbook, we knew it was a winner — great cover, great layout — and it looks comforting and substantial. I think our customers feel reassured when they pick it up — there's not many photos, but the text is so accessible, they feel confident that they can make the recipes themselves.'
Sydney Bookseller

'It's a pity when you read a great book, but it has a dreadful cover — it makes it twice as hard to sell.'
Adelaide Bookseller

How I got into production . . .

Here is how one person came to work in the area of production:

> *My current position is senior publishing consultant, Harcourt Brace, reporting to the managing director. Responsibilities: publishing (or acquisitions) editor with particular area of front list; also managing production while the production manager is on leave, and consultant on various publishing and production matters. How did I get into this? It was a mixture of Life, the Universe and Everything. I always wanted to illustrate children's books and started out doing that in South Africa, then took a digression through managing an art gallery, then digressed again to become manager of a flying school while acquiring a pilot's licence, at which time my intention was to become a commercial pilot.*
>
> *Then life took another meander and I went back to book design and illustration, and started editing too, probably because I was studying English at university at the time as an extra-mural student. Then, with two very small children, I moved to New Zealand and set up as a freelance editor and designer. This eventually became so busy that I set it up as a business, as a publishing consultancy, employing other freelancers and also taking on major contracts. Along the way, these included a period as publishing manager with Price Milburn, publishing fiction and non-fiction for children and teachers; and then a four-year period working on two special projects for the Publications Branch of the then Department of Education. I think they gave me the contract*

because it was so hideously complicated that an outsider might have more luck cutting through the red tape. The two projects were a mathematics program, which was simultaneously aimed at teachers and new-entrant school children, so publishing was at two very different levels; it involved books for teachers and illustrated card games for children. The other project involved the publication of parallel versions of Maori land legends in both Maori and English. A job to dream of!

When I moved to Australia in 1989, happenstance took me more in the direction of production for a while — production manager for Murdoch Books briefly, then production manager for OTEN, and then I moved to a senior management position at McGraw-Hill as manager of editorial and production services. I was there for just under five years.

Penny Martin, Senior Publishing Consultant, Harcourt Brace & Co.

6 Sales as a career

'Being a rep means no day is ever the same. I enjoy the challenge of juggling sales, relationships, budgets, promotion, mobile phones, lap-top computers, returns, new releases, back-list, and so many varied clients whilst constantly thinking about the next call.'
Linda O'Connell, (Ex)-Product Manager, Computing, Nelson ITP

'My first job was as a bookseller for the New Mint bookshop in Toorak. From there I worked for a variety of independent Melbourne bookshops for about ten years, and now I'm a sales rep for Tower Books. Tower represents a large number of publishers and we have a very wide variety of titles to sell in to booksellers, library suppliers and retailers. My territory is the City plus south-eastern Melbourne, Gippsland, Shepparton, Benalla and Warrnambool. I decided to become a sales rep as it was a natural progression from bookselling, you need similar skills and abilities to do the job well.'
Julie Maguire, Sales Representative, Tower Books

'It was luck that lead me to see an advertisement in the newspaper for a trade rep for Macmillan . . .'
Paula Hurley, Education Sales & Marketing Manager, Penguin Books Australia

'Every sales rep should spend at least six months working in a bookshop to understand how the rest of the trade works.'
Ex-Bookseller, now a Sales Manager

'I started out, like so many reps, as a bookseller. I think it's good to know how the customers think, and having worked in a bookshop for a couple of years, it gives you a real insight to what booksellers want from their suppliers.'
Sales Representative

'When I became a rep I couldn't believe it — no more dusting! But sorting out the returns make up for it.'
Anonymous Sales Representative

'I have the best job in the world! I love being on the road, visiting booksellers, library suppliers and other retail customers. It's very satisfying to build up a relationship with your booksellers and see how you can assist them to sell more of your range of books.'
Country Sales Representative

'Being a rep is quite a physical job. You are lugging around a trolley or suitcase on wheels full of books, in and out of your car, in and out of bookshops. I don't need to go to the gym as much now!'
Sales Representative

'I started off as a sales representative, and the experience was invaluable. That time spent selling in to bookshops means that when we have a new title proposal, I look at it and see what will work and what won't.'
Marketing Manager

'Sometimes it comes down to personality — I can teach someone about books and selling and how to be a good rep, but I can't teach them to love books and their customers.'
Training Manager

Sales representatives

Sales representatives are the communications pipeline between publisher and bookseller. Reps take the sample copies and new release information on the forthcoming books to bookshops, library and school suppliers and other retailers on a regular basis — usually once a month. As well as selling in the new list, reps check and authorise returns (booksellers are unable to send back damaged or old stock without a returns authorisation from the publisher or their representative), undertake a stock check to advise the bookseller of titles they have sold and may wish to reorder, as well as arranging of window and in-store displays, author events and promotions. They may visit a wide range of retailers, including small independent bookshops, large chains, department stores, university bookshops, library suppliers, speciality educational and school suppliers. Publishers often divide their sales departments into a number of areas — educational sales, special sales, trade sales and children's sales. To succeed in niche areas such as these, you need to have an excellent knowledge of the specialist field.

Working as a sales representative in educational sales can be quite different from working as a trade sales rep. For instance, you are often dealing with academics, seeking to have your titles placed on course reading and textbook lists. You will have to compete with a number of other publishers' sales reps who are trying to achieve the same aims, so knowing and understanding what the people who are assigning these lists really want is crucial. (Several years ago when I was searching for marketing texts for a course I was teaching, one publishing house offered me samples of the texts, plus a copy of each of the teacher's manuals. Its efforts to assist me were much appreciated and I eventually went with this publisher — not only were the texts excellent, but I felt that when it come to looking at texts for other subjects, this publisher would be helpful.)

An educational sales rep may attend educational and library conferences, as well as visiting academics on campus, in order to build up professional relationships and get a better knowledge of their industry.

The vision

Your employer has the most interesting of new and backlist titles for you to sell in, booksellers are always on time for their appointments (as are you!), offer you a cappuccino on a cold day or a cool drink on a stinking hot one. They always have allocated enough budget to buy lots of titles and are interested in your ideas for a promotion. Parking is a breeze, and you never get any tickets. Your sales manager has just told you that you are doing a great job

— lots of sales with minimal returns — and offers you a bonus over lunch!

The reality

You get six parking or speeding fines in a month, your mobile phone battery dies just as you get a flat on the highway on your way to see your biggest account. The books you have nobody wants to buy and the customers all mention the gruesome review your supposed best-seller got in the *Listener* and *Australian Book Review* last week. You have to visit four bookshops who take a whole hour to buy six books each and they don't offer you a coffee or the use of their washroom. You put your back out lugging the suitcase of books around, and, as you grab lunch at 3.30 p.m. (a sandwich in the car park) you wonder why you ever left bookselling.

7 Networking

'I'm a member of the APA, ABA and CBC. The smaller, more specific ones are especially valuable to hold membership within at various times of your career.'
Patricia Genat, Head of Division, ACER

'We (the company) are members of the Australian Booksellers Association. Any new staff who join our company now enrol for the ABA correspondence course. We currently have three people studying, have just enrolled two more and three more will enrol next month.'
Kevin Parken, Managing Director, Book Agencies of Adelaide

'I like the challenge, the variety and the contact with members.'
Rina Afflitto, Executive Director, Australian Booksellers Association

'The APA provides a valuable forum to voice opinions and initiate change.'
Belinda Bolliger, Children's Publisher, Hodder Headline

'It is important to join appropriate industry bodies and participate in their activities to maintain contact and influence decisions that may affect the industry as a whole. I have always

found booksellers in particular are very happy to share information and offer assistance.'
Jean Ferguson, Book Industry Consultant, Member of ABA and CBC

'The industry associations are important — they educate, mobilise and offer camaraderie.'
Nick Walker, Director, Australian Scholarly Publishing, Member of APA

'The APA, Society of Editors, Pen International and Australian Society of Authors.'
Ray Coffey, Publisher, Fremantle Arts Centre Press

'Trade knowledge is invaluable — no matter where you get, you must network.'
Sales & Marketing Director

'I belong to the Public Relations Institute of Australia, the Publicity Group (Sydney) and the APA.'
Christine Farmer, National Publicity Manager, HarperCollins

'They are useful to provide networks and a wide range of ideas. Also, they can achieve things that an individual in the industry cannot, such as lobbying government.'
Jo Breese, Chief Executive Officer, New Zealand Booksellers Association

'I'm a fellow of the Institute for Engineers Australia and also belong to the Eastern Suburbs Personnel and Industrial Groups, which, like other trade organisations, can be of value for such purposes as networking, exchanging knowledge and gaining ideas.'
Ron Caithness, Operations Manager, Penguin Books Australia

'We belong to Publish Australia and the Australian Book Group, the latter of which is working very hard to improve the business (especially book sales) of its members.'
Stephanie Johnston, Director, Wakefield Press

'Essential to join.'
David Gaunt, Co-proprietor, Gleebooks, Member of ABA and CBC

Why network?

There is an old saying that 'it's who you know that will get you an interview and what you know that will get you the job'. Word of mouth is one of the most powerful methods of finding work. The publishing profession and bookselling industries in Australia and New Zealand are relatively small when compared with those in the UK or USA, and it is very much a case of everyone knowing of or knowing someone who knows everyone else. Therefore, it is to your advantage to meet and make contact with as many and as wide a variety of people as possible. Beware: networking is not about doing a smash and grab, it is about relationship building. The sales representative you meet today may be a sales manager or marketing director in the future. The editorial assistant or receptionist may end up production manager or permissions editor, the bookseller you rudely snub or berate at the conference may turn up as marketing manager or newspaper reviewer of your title tomorrow! This does not mean putting on a false persona and being gushingly nice, it simply means that you treat people with respect and should, whenever the opportunity presents itself, introduce yourself and ask the other person to tell you about their work and themselves. As talking about themselves is most people's favourite subject, this should pose no problem! In all seriousness, however, the trade being so small, everyone does get to hear pretty much what is going on. Don't play the fool when you attend industry events, keep that for your personal time. You want to be remembered as that intelligent person with the computer diploma who loves travel books whom they met at the book launch and who may suit the publishing assistant position coming up, not the idiot who made smart remarks to the author to show off.

If you are new to the idea of publishing as a profession, there are some good special interest groups that you can join, and many of these run excellent training courses — these are listed with full contact details in Chapter 12. As soon as you are eligible, join the professional organisation that covers your interest. Benefits of joining these organisations include:

- access to valuable contacts who can guide you, pass on information and discuss interest and similar issues and problems that you face
- notification of excellent and timely training courses run by their and other organisations through meetings, newsletters and word of mouth. These courses tend to be run by experienced, knowledgeable members of the organisation
- the chance to meet members of the association and committee members who should themselves have excellent networks
- receipt of newsletter and membership directory that will contain information of interest to your profession
- looks good on your CV, as it shows that you take your intended profession seriously enough to join the professional body associated with your area of interest
- invitations to social events such as annual dinners (where you can meet members), and monthly meetings which may take the form of a dinner with a guest speaker and seminars and conferences
- tax-deductible membership charges, as well as any training courses/seminars and conferences that you attend under their auspices.

PROFESSION	ORGANISATION
Bookselling	Australian Booksellers Association
	Booksellers New Zealand
	Christian Booksellers Association of Australia
	Christian Booksellers Association of New Zealand
Children's books	Children's Book Council
	Children's Literature Association of New Zealand Inc.
	New Zealand Children's Book Foundation
Design	Australian Book Designers' Group
Editing	Society of Editors
	New Zealand Book Editors' Association
Indexing	Society of Indexers
Literature	National Book Council, Australia
	New Zealand Book Council

Production	The Galley Club
You are female	Women in Publishing
	Listener Women's Book Festival
Writing	Australian Society of Authors
	Writers Centre in your state, Australia
	New Zealand Reading Association
	New Zealand Writers Guild
	New Zealand Society of Authors (Pen NZ Inc.)

Meeting people

Whenever you meet someone at an industry gathering (book launch, training course, conference or seminar) ask them for a business card. This will allow you to maintain a growing database of contacts. As soon as you can after meeting that person, write down on the back of the card, the date and the circumstances where you met. It also means, of course, that you have an accurate record of their name, position title and company, should you need to contact them later. This is useful so that if in three months' time you want to apply for a position in their company, you could contact them and ask them for information about the company or if they have any ideas of how you could improve your chances. They may also be impressed that you remember when you met them and it will assist you in keeping in touch with your contact.

Remember to give as well as take. If you simply try to get as much as you can from your networking, without giving any assistance in return, you will not (nor will you deserve to) get very far. Networking and relationship building are a two-way street. Say you have met the HR officer of a publishing house at the book fair, and then in two weeks' time you see an article on headhunters in the newspaper, you clip the article and send it to her saying you thought it might be of interest.

Other ways to make contacts

You don't need to wait to meet people face to face. You could telephone or write to the author of an article that interested you in a trade journal or newsletter; or telephone a publishing house and ask the receptionist for the name of the person who manages or works in the area of your interest. Call them and ask if you can meet them at their convenience for a coffee for fifteen minutes to ask them a few questions. Or you could make contact with a staff member of a professional organisation that covers your interest, and request that they suggest a few people for you to call. Thus, you have instant access to a network.

How to network

Here are some tips to make your networking effective:

- Always ask your new acquaintance for their business card and fill in the details of your meeting on the back after the event.
- Get yourself a business card to hand out in return. It may simply have your name and the words 'Book Editing position wanted', plus your address and telephone number. Many printers have a limited number of styles that are quite inexpensive. To keep your cards pristine, not covered in lipstick from your handbag or bent from your wallet, invest in an inexpensive metal or leather business card holder.
- Contact the person you met a few days later and suggest meeting for a coffee or forward the article or material that you promised in your conversation. Always ask them to suggest someone else with whom you can speak. Then you are able to call and say, 'Good morning John Martin, Jane Smith at Penguin gave me your name and said I should call you to find out about DTP — is now a good time to talk?'
- At appropriate times, such as morning tea at a training seminar, talk to the people next to you. Introduce yourself to the people running the event, and request that they put you on their mailing list for the future. Ask them if they would introduce you to the speaker, for example. Make an effort — you can't afford to be shy and self-conscious at these events.
- When you meet other people in the same situation as yourself, agree to pool resources. Not every position that comes along will suit you and vice versa. It is also good

to have someone to discuss your job hunt with, especially if that person is in the same boat and understands exactly what you are hoping to find.

- When you call someone, always ask if it is a convenient time to speak. They may be in a meeting or working to deadline and not want to take time then, so they will appreciate your good manners.

- Ask relevant questions when the opportunity arises. If you don't understand something the speaker is talking about, then ask. Better to ask than pretend you understand something you don't and be caught out as an idiot!

- Personal presentation is important. Although in-house publishing staff are generally not known for their fashion, make sure you wear neat and tidy clothing appropriate for the event. You want to project a capable and mature appearance. Wearing old jeans and a T-shirt might mean you will be thought to want the job in the warehouse rather than in-house.

- Don't drink too much. This may sound pretty obvious, but at many social events such as book launches, there will be plenty of drinks available. I was once asked by a good friend to take an acquaintance of his, an aspiring author, to the Victorian Premier's Literary Awards Announcement launch, and the fellow proceeded to drink about six glasses of wine as soon as we got there! Not an auspicious start, as there was then no way I was going to introduce him to any of the publishers there, and as I felt his behaviour as my guest was dreadful, I would never assist him again.

Finding out about networking events

Most industry events in Australia will appear in the *Weekly Book Newsletter* (*WBN*). In New Zealand the *Booksellers News*, the *Publisher*, and the newsletter of the Society of Authors are all good sources of information. The *WBN* is an invaluable newsletter which appears 50 times a year and carries information on everything from book rights bought and sold, personnel changes, authors on tour, books being promoted, literary festivals, training and very importantly, job vacancies. For the last reason alone, some organisations don't allow their staff to see issues for some time or even go so far as to remove the job pages! It may be worthwhile to invest in a subscription of your own. Some of the events you should be able to attend without too much trouble are:

- Book launches — Ask your local bookshops to let you know when they are hosting any book launches and to place you on their mailing/customer list.
- Training seminars — These will probably be advertised in the *Weekly Book Newsletter* as well as the professional organisations newsletters in Australia and New Zealand.
- APA Book Fair — Held in Sydney every year in August, but due to move to Melbourne in 1998. This is the publishing industry's annual trade fair. As well as seminars and launches, the majority of Australian and international publishers and distributors and their staff get together to display current backlist and new releases. Well worth a look.
- The annual Booksellers Association conference in New Zealand is a good meeting place for publishers and booksellers. The Listener Women's Book Festival is an annual event that happens around the country. It is hoped to have a Book Expo in New Zealand in 1998.

Word of mouth

Ask around — you may be surprised who knows who in publishing. One of my work experience students made a contact through her mother's hairdresser's sister, who turned out to be the State Sales Manager for one of the biggest Australian publishers. A colleague met a shy woman at a book launch who turned out to be one of Australia's award-winning writers. Tell all your friends and family your career intentions and there is a chance that someone will know someone, and it would be foolish not to use the opportunity.

Summary of networking

- Attend as many different literary/industry events as you can to ascertain which groups best suit you.
- Remember that networking is about relationships — you need to give as well as receive to be a success. If you are perceived as a 'taker' only, you will not succeed.
- Once you decide to join a group — don't delay!

- OK, now you are a member, get involved. Volunteer to assist on the newsletter, organise meetings, arrange for events. This will be enjoyable as well as knowledge building.
- Introduce yourself to as many people as possible.
- Collect business cards.
- Organise a business card yourself, perhaps it will have 'Publishing position wanted' printed on it. Certainly it must have your name and contact details clearly printed. Make sure you project the image you want.
- Tell friends, relatives, other people you come into contact with that you are looking for a job in a specific area. Don't just say in publishing, that is too broad, give a focused description, such as editing, production, bookselling or copyright.
- Join local organisations such as writers' groups, book clubs and libraries and general book trade organisations, such as the Australian Booksellers Association, the New Zealand Society of Authors, New Zealand Book Council, National Book Council, Children's Book Council or the Galley Club.
- Read trade journals and newsletters, book review pages in the daily newspapers, special interest group notices and if you can't afford to buy, then borrow the titles listed in Chapter 13.

8 The résumé

'Candidates must think very carefully about the job for which they are applying. I've seen too many CVs that have information about personal pursuits (appearances in school plays and so on) that bear no relevance to the job and an equally large number that underplay experiences which might bring organisational and/or literary skills to light.'
Andrew Watson, Assistant Director, Melbourne University Press

'Include in your résumé your transferable skills — for example, strong communication (including writing) skills. Any extra-curricular activities which show that a candidate has a genuine interest in all/any aspects of the publishing industry.'
Michelle Atkins, Copyright and Permissions Editor/Contracts Controller/Primary Editor, Nelson ITP

'Don't include that you love to read, by all means mention that you do read, but do not give the impression that you would read all day. Don't tell me that you are a budding or hopeful author.'
Peter Milne, Deputy Managing Director, Abbey's Bookshops

Your résumé and accompanying cover letter are some of the most important documents you will ever produce. They have to represent you, speak on your behalf and convincingly communicate your strengths, skills, experience and potential, so the résumé must be clear, impressive and professional in appearance and content. By reading your cover letter and résumé, the potential employer should be able to ascertain whether or not they wish to interview you for the position. Your application needs to assure the employer that you can handle the job.

In short, a vacancy is really a headache for the company. Sure, it is also an opportunity for them to bring in someone with good skills, appropriate experience and great ideas, but it can also be a stressful exercise for them to choose the right person. Your job is to do your best to assure them that you are the right person.

In some publishing houses or bookshops, there will be no one person handling the human resource function as a full-time position. Therefore, while the person who is reading and assessing the applications will in all probability have an excellent idea of the work required and the type of person they want, they may lack experience or confidence in their ability to do the hiring process. This means that you have to make it easy for them! By demonstrating in your cover letter and résumé that you can undertake the position, your application will stand out amongst all the others.

On the other hand, when you are in contact with a Human Resource manager, they may have a different approach, perhaps one that is slightly more formal. But the same principle applies — make your application the one they cannot ignore.

As soon as you cut out the advertisement or hear about the vacancy, ring up the appropriate person and request (if there is time before the application closure date) that they fax or mail you a copy of the position description. This will ensure that you cover every important point, as they may not all be emphasised in the advertisement.

This is also a good opportunity to find out the name of the person to whom you should address the cover letter. Nothing is more annoying than receiving a 'Dear Mr or Madam letter', especially if the advertisement to which you are responding has a name indicated. If you are unsure of the spelling or job title, or it does say forward to the HR Manager, ask them or the receptionist for their name and the correct spelling.

Also get as much information as you can concerning the company. Look through back issues of trade magazines, if it is a publishing house, then look at their titles in bookshops. If it is a bookshop, then dress appropriately and pay an anonymous visit yourself to check them out. Talk to friends and contacts that you may have in order to collect more data. Use the library. Does the company have a website?

The cover letter

The aim of the cover letter is to get the employer or human resource manager to look at your résumé and feel enthusiastic about your application and potential as an interviewee. The cover letter should convey the following:

- your interest in the position and the company
- your ability to successfully undertake the required responsibilities and duties
- previous experience you might have in a similar role
- knowledge and awareness of the book trade and where and how the company fits into this industry
- your experience and ability in the particular areas specified in the advertisement — don't just rave on about your abilities. If the advertisement or position description says that word processing or data entry or sales is a component, then indicate how you can satisfy these requirements.

Cover letters should be kept to one page, unless you are applying for a senior position and you have the experience, qualifications and skills that require a more in-depth approach.

Apply for the job advertised, do not say in an application for a sales rep job that you want to be an editor or production assistant. Publishers and booksellers do not want people who want to do other things working for them. Like other managers, they want people who want to be doing the job they are employed to do working for them. The employer may be concerned that you will leave as soon as your dream job comes up. Certainly, employers are keen for their staff to be ambitious and in some cases they do promote people internally to other areas, but if the position advertised is for a receptionist or sales representative or bookseller or proofreader, then apply for just that!

Always find out to whom you should address the cover letter. If you are unsure of the spelling or job title, ring the company and ask the receptionist.

The opening paragraph should grab the reader's attention and make them read on. The following example worked very well for me when I was job hunting and it must still be OK as I regularly see variations on it sent into Bookstaff: 'I was delighted to see your advertisement for Job X as it is just the position I have been looking for and for the following reasons, I am sure that I would be an ideal candidate.'

Show an interest in the company and illustrate that you do know something about their publications or business.

The résumé

The résumé should be composed of six parts appearing in the following order:
1 personal contact details
2 skills, strengths and abilities
3 industry exposure and knowledge
4 education
5 career/work experience details
6 referees.

1 Personal contact details

Always include and spell out your first and last name. Don't include your middle name or initial unless you always include these when signing letters or your name. Please ensure that you spell your name correctly — I have had numerous cases where no doubt nervousness has caused keystroke errors.

Make sure that the contact numbers you provide are up to date and correct. If you have an answering machine at home, ensure it contains a business-like message — no funny or weird messages as these will not impress your potential employer. Also a no-no are long pieces of music. I once gave up trying to contact a candidate for an entry-level position because I could not endure a 30-second cut from 'Smoke on the Water'. It was easier to interview the candidates whose machines simply invited me to leave my name and number.

2 Skills, strengths and abilities

Make sure there is a heading for skills on your résumé. Include strengths such as communication, time management, computer literacy (list all programs), organisation, other languages, and abilities relevant to the job application. This is not a time to be modest — no-one else will say how good you are. A good candidate knows and, in a professional and confident manner, states their skills.

3 Industry exposure and knowledge

This is where you place your professional memberships, workshops, training, events, conferences and seminars. Include information regarding trade journals subscriptions, such as *Weekly Book Newsletter*, *Booksellers News* (New Zealand), the *Publisher* (New Zealand), *Australian Bookseller & Publisher* and *Australian Book Review*. If you have attended book launches, author readings and signings, literary festivals, they also go under this heading.

4 Education

Always place your education in reverse chronological order. Don't include a breakdown of individual subjects: the fact that you received 87% for English Literature is less important than the fact that you have passed your Bachelor of Arts.

Set out any industry education — seminars, classes, night school or special courses, in addition to your formal secondary or tertiary study.

If you have undertaken advanced study, such as a PhD, you may prefer to play down these educational achievements so that potential employers will not consider you 'over qualified'.

5 Career/work experience details

This is crucial information. You must use positive language which has the ring of success to it. Use words such as 'managed', 'achieved', 'created', 'implemented', 'saved money', 'increased sales', 'met deadlines early' to let the reader know that you didn't just do what you had to, you contributed more.

Make sure that you don't set out a virtual position description in huge details for each job, simply give a sentence or two detail of the company's background and list in point form the position you held and what the main responsibilities were/are.

The fact you have undertaken unpaid work experience is almost always looked upon favourably. It shows that you have determination to get out there and make things happen, rather than wait for someone to hand you an opportunity.

6 Referees

Written references should not be included since most interviewers will prefer to call your previous employers and lecturers instead. Candidates only show you the good references (if they have any sense!), so I always prefer to speak with their direct supervisors, co-workers and managers.

Make sure that the contact details are up to date: it is frustrating if the referee has left their previous position five months earlier and the interviewer has to chase them up, a fact which will reflect poorly on the candidate.

Be sure of your referee! Contact them prior to your application and ask if they would feel comfortable being a referee. If you detect any hint of a refusal, then don't put them in. You want to be confident that your referee will give you a glowing account, not a lukewarm response.

Do warn them that they may be contacted. There is nothing worse than being on the hop and trying to remember which of the summer work experience people the interviewer is calling about, as the referee may be frantically busy with lots of tasks and unintentionally make it seem as though they cannot remember who you are, let alone if you did a great job as a production assistant.

Do . . .

- Tailor your résumé for every job for which you apply. Your skills and abilities grow and improve over time, so your résumé must reflect this.
- Highlight and reinforce relevant experience.

- Make your résumé easy to follow. The best experience and skills in the world will not get you an interview if your application cannot communicate these facts.
- Place all work in chronological order starting with the most recent, unless a particular position you held some time ago is very relevant to the position for which you are applying.
- Place all study in chronological order starting with the most recent, unless a course or degree you did some time ago is very relevant to the position for which you are applying.
- Use the computer spell and grammar checker several times!
- Print out a copy of your cover letter and résumé in order to pick up any mistakes or keystroke errors you may have missed on the screen. Then ask another person to cast their eye over this. Often you will be too close to the creation of the documents to be able to suggest important corrections.
- Address the letter to a name and position, never to a position only.
- Include references, and allocate them to the Professional, Academic and Personal categories.
- Include samples of reviews/publication lists/awards etc. that are relevant.
- Keep up to date in your area of speciality — when you attend courses, read relevant articles, join professional organisations, list them in your résumé.
- Use appropriate language; don't use jargon! Even if you are applying for an Information Technology job where acronyms abound, your application should be able to be read or initially assessed by someone who is not a technophile! As communication is a key skill that every position requires, you may be unintentionally putting yourself out of the running.
- Do be honest. At Bookstaff, as at many other companies, we check up everything: work experience, positions held, work attitude and academic qualifications.
- Do number your pages. It may have to be photocopied or faxed on, and this will make it easier to collate.

Don't

- Forget to check spelling and grammar. I am always amazed how many poorly spelt applications are sent to me for book trade positions.
- Ramble on about unimportant or unrelated issues. The employer does not want to know about your holiday plans, child-rearing experiences or family crises.
- Include unnecessary information — if you have a tertiary qualification then there is no need to include your high school information.
- Include details of subjects studied in your academic results.
- Include records of any primary school attendance or study. It is assumed that you have attended primary school.
- Include secondary school information, such as being a prefect or exchange student when you were fourteen. If you are over 25, it is no longer relevant.
- Bind your résumé as this makes it difficult to photocopy in the case of a panel interview or selection committee. A single staple or paperclip is fine.
- Use small or large printing — 11 or 12 point is best.
- Use too many fonts — two is the maximum.
- Use dark-coloured or overly textured paper as this is difficult to photocopy or read.
- Over-design your résumé.
- Lie — in these days of careful employment, potential employers are more carefully checking references, work and education records.
- List too many or very weird hobbies or interests.
- Use pretentious fonts. Stick to something simple such as Times New Roman, Ariel or Palatino.
- Print your résumé on anything but a laser or very good bubble jet printer — dot matrix is out!

The employer's point of view

Here are what a variety of book industry employers would like to see included in your résumé and/or cover letter:

'I would want to know that applicants have computer ability and some indication that they are quick on the uptake and

capable of using their own initiative — especially important for production jobs'.
Andrew Watson, Assistant Director, Melbourne University Press

'The candidate's degree of computer literacy — packages known, experiences with people and deadlines. Interests outside the workplace.'
Patricia Genat, Head of Division, ACER

'The usual: educational history and achievements, career paths with dates, previous held. All jobs — waiting, car washing etc. — to be included. Details of outside interests, activities. Personal attributes relevant to the job.'
Tony Davies, Deputy Director, Cambridge University Press

'Knowledge of computers. Some keyboard skills. Willingness to take responsibility.'
Kevin Parken, Managing Director, Book Agencies of Adelaide

'In a detailed CV I would want to see details of experience the applicant has had in the book industry. But many people who don't have experience still want to break into the book trade (like me, once upon a time . . .) In that case, what I would like to see are some details on the type of activities that bear some similarity to the book trade — such as volunteer work on newsletters and similar publications, computer skills and organisational skills — or activities that show the applicant is adaptable and flexible when it comes to learning new skills. I would also be looking for signs of passion for the industry. A person who is trying to 'break in', and who is taking short courses on publishing, attending writer's festivals and conferences (and that type of thing) would be more likely to succeed than someone who simply states they would like to work with books.'
Carolyn Leslie, Editor, Non-fiction, HarperCollins

'Five-year goal(s). Proven reliability (if possible). Health. Complete employment history with dates and contact phone numbers.'
Barbara Cullen, General Manager and Director, Page One

'Work experience, special skills and to get a feel of the personality.'
Jo Breese, CEO, Booksellers Association of New Zealand

'Skills, ideas, enthusiasm. Why you should get the job'.
Christine Farmer, National Publicity Manager, HarperCollins

'Specific projects and your role(s) in them: awards; interests and passions; committee membership; educational and employment details.'
Deborah Doyle, Freelance Book Editor and Teacher

'With regard to the job, I want honest answers about skills. Not too much embellishing. Job aside, I like the juicy bits, like "I worked on a yacht with Omar Sharif sailing around the Mediterranean".'
Kristen Baragwanath, Acquisitions Editor, Schools Division, McGraw-Hill

'Informed career goals; so few seem to be thought through.'
Lucie Pepeyan, Manager, General Book Department, McGills

'Work experience, computer packages you know, educational experience and types of books you read with examples.'
Peter Milne, Deputy Managing Director, Abbey's Bookshops

And here are a variety of book industry employers saying what **not** to include in a résumé:

'Details of physical and mental breakdown. Never say "I love books".'
Tony Davies, Deputy Director, Cambridge University Press

'I love books and I want to read all of them.'
Kevin Parken, Managing Director, Book Agencies of Adelaide

'Don't include that you love to read, by all means mention that you do read, but do not give the impression that you would read all day. Don't tell me that you are a budding or hopeful author.'
Peter Milne, Deputy Managing Director, Abbey's Bookshops

'If you are applying for a bookselling position, don't state that you want to work in publishing — it implies that you will leave ASAP a publishing job becomes available.'
Lucie Pepeyan, Manager, General Book Department, McGills

'Failed or unfinished courses of study.'
Jane Routley, Freelance Writer, author of Mage Heart

'Untransferable skills. Also, if you have a legal background downplay it. Interviewers may be suspicious of anyone leaving the glamourous world of LA Law.'
Michelle Atkins, Copyright and Permissions Editor/Contracts Controller/Primary Editor, Nelson ITP

'Copious amounts of irrelevant references.'
Barbara Cullen, General Manager and Director, Page One

'Too much detail can be off-putting.'
Jo Breese, CEO, Booksellers New Zealand

'In your CV, if you apply for a publicity job, but indicate that you want to be an 'editor' . . . don't. Apply your résumé to the job at hand. Don't say "I write books". Too romantic.'
Christine Farmer, National Publicity Manager, HarperCollins

'Any jobs that lasted less than three months; personal failures; date of birth if you're over forty.'
Deborah Doyle, Freelance Book Editor and Teacher

'Where they went to primary school! Keep your CV succinct and relevant.'
Kristen Baragwanath, Acquisitions Editor, Schools Division, McGraw-Hill

A sample résumé is presented on the next page.

Résumé
BOOKSTAFF SAMPLE SUGGESTED LAYOUT

Charlotte Brontë

Address: 45 Haywood Parish Road, Richmond,
                  Victoria 3121
Telephone: 03 9999 9999
Age: 24 *(Only indicate your age if under 30)*
Aim: *(Tailor this aim for every different position*
                  for which you apply)
                  To gain an entry-level position in editing
                  within the publishing industry.

Skills

- *Verbal and written communication skills:* I am able to
  effectively and efficiently communicate with a variety of
  people.
- *Computer Literate:* I am computer literate in Microsoft
  Word for Windows, Excel and Lotus applications.
- *Multi-lingual:* I can speak Japanese

Book Trade experience

- Attended 'Introduction to Book Publishing' course at
  XYZ during 1997

- Worked full-time as a bookseller at Waterstones for three
  years

- Work experience with John Smith, Editor, Serious Publications Ltd

Academic Qualifications

Graduate Diploma in Marketing, Wherever TAFE, 1996

Research and projects on direct-mail marketing and retail
displays

Bachelor of Arts, Australian National University, 1992–1996

Majors in Slavonic Literature and Ancient Hellenic Epic

Memberships

Galley Club

Victorian Writers' Centre

CAE Book group

Career Experience

1992–1995, Sales Assistant, Waterstones Booksellers
Duties included: Customer service, dealing with complaints and enquiries, maintenance of customer database, general administrative duties.

May 1994, Work experience, John Smith, Editor, Serious Publications
Duties included: General administrative tasks involving filing, faxing and using Microsoft Word for Windows and Excel computer packages.

1984–1994, Waitress, Conran Cafe

References
Employment: John Smith
Editor
Serious Publications
Tel: (W) 9666 5656

Jane Austen
Owner
Amora
Romance Bookshop
Tel: (W) 9666 6565

Sally Midriff
Former Supervisor
Waterstones Bookshop
Currently: Director
Midriff Book Publishers
Tel: (W) 9665 5665

Academic: Professor Charles Dickens
               Supervisor, Graduate Diploma
               Australian National University
               Tel: (W) 026 2565 5665

If you are more senior in experience, you may choose to set
out your CV in this manner:

Page 1   Cover Page
Page 2   Personal Details (name, address, telephone, aim,
          skills, education, memberships, interests)
Pages3–5 Career Experience
Page 6   References

9 Excelling at the interview

'The job applicant has to show me they want the job and that in terms of their career, this job "makes sense". Otherwise I will be very curious about their motivation for applying and have doubts about their intention to stay if they are selected. This doesn't mean that people can't transfer from different fields and in that case I would advise them to show that their skills are transferable and again, that they have done their research in terms of this new field.

'Basically, if you're looking for a job, you need to make it as easy as possible for someone to select you. This means doing a lot of work on your part such as researching the company and the position, submitting an application that spells out exactly why you are the most suitable candidate for the job, and adapting your CV to show that your previous experience, skills and education are relevant for this job. Don't expect the people responsible for hiring to make the links — you need to do that for them. If you're not prepared to put a decent amount of effort into job applications and interviews, I would almost have to tell you not to bother at all. Unless you have skills that are rare and in demand, the job market is so competitive you will be wasting your time if you put in mediocre applications and turn up to interviews without doing any preparation.'
Susan Ainsworth, HR Consultant and Lecturer in Management and Human Resources, RMIT

'Our company has examined the key selection criteria required

for each position level. There are up to 16 key selection criteria
that we evaluate. These range from position level to position
level. A standard interview guide that examines the relevant
selection criteria is the basis for an interview with each candidate. This enables us to make objective decisions about
candidates and select the right person for the job each time.'
Rochelle Anderson, HR Manager, Collins Booksellers

'Research the company you would like to work for — it's very
impressive at the interview.'
*Abigail Freeman, Human Resource Manager, Addison Wesley
Longman*

Congratulations — you have an interview!

While the interview can be a time of great stress, it is also
a time of great opportunity. Here is your chance to show
the interviewer why you are the best person for the position.
Look upon the interview as a chance to showcase your
talents and abilities. We are often brought up to be well
behaved and not show off, but an interview is exactly the
time to do just that. It is not a time to be modest and hide
your light under a bushel. If you are good at customer
service, sales, editing, juggling a dozen tasks, meeting
deadlines, proofing documents, liaising with printers — this
is the time to say so!

Baden Powell said it the best: Be prepared! I am often
appalled by the number of people whom I interview who
have no real idea of what kind of books the company they
are applying to work for actually publishes or sells. It shows
a complete lack of awareness, interest and initiative. A
candidate who can demonstrate that they have researched
their prospective employer indicates that they have enthusiasm and intelligence, and they have passed the first
milestone in the interview.

When they call you to arrange the interview always ask
if this is a panel interview. If there will be more than one
person, ask for their names and position titles. You can then
bone up on their backgrounds and learn their names so you
won't forget them during the interview.

Now is the time to ask for a copy of the position
description if you don't already have one. This will allow

you to carefully check that you can undertake all the duties and fulfil the range of responsibilities expected and probably not spelled out fully in the original advertisement.

If you are unfamiliar with the company and have tried without success to locate any documentation, request that they forward you a copy of any catalogues. Say something like 'I've read through *Booksellers News* and checked out the local bookshops and library, but I would still like to see a copy of your latest catalogue — could you please forward one to me?'

Confirm with the caller the interview time, date and address and write them down. Often in the excitement, people mistake times and dates and nothing gives a worse impression than turning up at the wrong date and time!

How to shine at the interview

Be confident. These days when everyone is busy, the interviewer would not be interested in wasting their time and yours by calling you in if they did not believe that you were any good.

Know something about the company: comb trade journals, speak with friends and contacts, so that you go in with some understanding about what they publish or retail. This is where your time spent on research (visiting libraries, reading trade journals, scouring the Internet, speaking with people in the profession and reading relevant books) will stand you in good stead.

Take a spare CV. The original may have jammed in the photocopier, got stuck in the fax, been a victim of a cup of spilled coffee. If you know that you are facing a panel interview, take along enough copies for each person.

Present well. Wear appropriate clothing and accessories.

Know the position description thoroughly and have an example of how you would or have previously handled each of the tasks required.

Ask questions. You should consider the interview as an opportunity for you to discover if this is the type of company for which you want to work. Write down the questions, so that in the heat of the moment you don't forget them. If the interviewer answers all of your questions during the time they are explaining the position and company background to you, still pull out your notepad, scan the questions and say, 'I think you have answered all the questions I was going to ask' to let them know that you did have some.

Don't ask about salary, annual leave, sick pay or other perks until the interviewer brings them up. You should, through your research, be aware of the salary level appropriate for this position; it may even be listed on the position description. It is poor form to ask about these issues straight away (as is reflected in the two quotes below). You should go into the interview knowing the salary range that covers this position so that you are able to negotiate the appropriate level that takes in to consideration your experience and abilities.

'If the first thing a candidate does is ask about the salary, then I know they are not the right person for us.'
Production Manager

'If they are too concerned with the money and not enough with the job, that does not give us a good impression of how seriously they will take their work. It also leads us to think that they will leave when a job comes along that pays more.'
HR Consultant

Successful characteristics

The most important characteristics that successful candidates display in interviews are:

'Initiative, enthusiasm and dedication.'
Rina Afflitto, Executive Director, Australian Booksellers Association

'Confidence, desire to work with the company and the ability to speak openly.'
Abigail Freeman, Human Resources Manager, Addison Wesley Longman

'Loads of enthusiasm and healthy self-image.'
Benny Belbin, Sales & Marketing Manager, Capricorn Link

'Passion for reading and books.'
Mary Howell, Sales and Marketing Director, Hodder Headline

'Enthusiasm and personality.'
Caroline Radford, Managing Director, Sales & Marketing, Technical Book & Magazine Company

'Confidence.'
Fiona Inglis, Literary Agent, Curtis Brown (Australia)

'Confidence (without arrogance) in their abilities.'
Lynne Spender, Executive Director, Australian Society of Authors

'Communication skills.'
Jean Ferguson, Book Industry Consultant

'Confidence.'
Ian Tucker, General Manager STMP Division, Harcourt Brace & Co.

'An example of passion and power over single project.'
Dennis Jones, Director, Dennis Jones & Associates

'Strong and appealing personal skills.'
Michelle Atkins, Copyright & Permissions Editor, Nelson ITP

'Confidence — if the applicant has this as well as some of the appropriate skills in the required area, they're half way there.'
Penny Martin, Senior Publishing Consultant, Harcourt Brace & Co.

'Focus.'
Louis de Vries, Manager, AGPS Victoria

'A calm, friendly manner goes a long way to reassuring you that that you are making the right decision.'
Kristen Baragwanath, Acquisitions Editor, Schools Division, McGraw-Hill

'Confidence in their ability to meet and exceed the selection criteria.'
Deborah Doyle, Freelance Book Editor and Lecturer

'They are well read, have a sense of humour and (very important) can work under pressure.'
Carolyn Leslie, Editor, Non-fiction, HarperCollins

'At interview, a really good candidate is prepared — they have thought about the work of the position and have intelligent questions to ask the panel — this is where the research pays off. It says a lot about the kind of person you are if you have gone to this kind of trouble and it is very easy to detect. Of course the person should be well presented, know their own job application backwards and be able to give examples to illustrate how suitable they are for the job. In addition to their

technical capability I would nearly always be looking for someone who fits not only the job but also the company culture, otherwise they are not likely to be satisfied and will probably leave within a short period of time. The ability to communicate and relate to other people is another "given" regardless of the job. You also need to demonstrate this at interview: everyone gets nervous, but you need to work hard to convey the impression that you are comfortable with people and confident about your own abilities.'
Susan Ainsworth, HR Consultant and Lecturer in Management and Human Resources, RMIT

'An interest in the job, either they have researched it well already, or have some reasonable questions to ask — especially of how their skills can match their job requirements.'
Patricia Genat, Head of Division, ACER

'Self-confidence — even the ability to say "I don't know the answer to that". No point in bluffing: give full and honest answers.'
Jeremy Fisher, General Manager, Tertiary Division, McGraw-Hill

'Mental agility.'
Andrew Watson, Assistant Director, Melbourne University Press

'Enthusiasm and likeability.'
Peter Donoughue, Managing Director, Jacaranda Wiley

'Asking the right questions.'
Stephanie Johnston, Director, Wakefield Press

'Initiative.'
Belinda Bolliger, Children's Publisher, Hodder Headline

'Depth of knowledge in their area, or the ability to think strategically and thereby be able to work things out.'
Susan Hawthorne, Publisher and Director, Spinifex Press

'Self-motivation and initiative.'
Ray Coffey, Publisher, Fremantle Arts Press

'Motivation which is belief in yourself — not arrogance.'
Helen Elliott, Book Editor, Herald-Sun

'Enthusiasm: with the right attitude you can do anything.'
Lucie Pepeyan, Manager, General Book Department, McGills

'A certain self-confidence coupled with intelligent answers and questions.'
Peter Milne, Deputy Managing Director, Abbey's Bookshops

'Crossing the divide — making me believe that they're not just interested in the book trade for the usual reasons, i.e. can't think of anything bad about it and it sounds interesting. Passion for books and people skills in retail are essential.'
David Gaunt, Co-proprietor, Gleebooks

'Honesty, openness and a desire to learn.'
Jo Breese, CEO, Booksellers New Zealand

Presentation

'You never get a second chance to make a first impression.'
Proverb

'I have had the occasional person say "This is how I am, I'm not going to change my appearance for anyone". Well, my answer is "Do you really want this job?"'
Senior HR Consultant

'Looking like the person who can do the job is half the battle.'
Administration Manager

'We are not going to choose the best groomed or dressed person, but if the applicant can show that they appear professional, it certainly won't go against them in the interview.'
HR Consultant

You don't have to rush out and spend a lot of money, but in order to give yourself the best opportunity, your personal presentation has to be excellent. There is great confidence in knowing your presentation is good — it allows you to relax about your appearance and get on with showing the interviewer why you are the best person for the job.

Remember that while not every publishing house will have the same dress code, first impressions count! If you are going for an interview at Lonely Planet, then the dress code is likely to be more relaxed than at a university press. Some professions dress differently from others: editors, for example, often have a more relaxed style than sales and marketing staff who have a great deal of client or media contact. In bookshops, the chain bookshops are often more conservative than the independent bookshops, Dymocks for example have a uniform which all of their staff wear — this does not make them better or worse, just different. If you research the style of the company you can't go wrong. If all else fails, a classic navy suit should cover most situations!

Some of the following items may seem obvious, but any HR Manager will notice if you have got them wrong in an interview:

- *Deodorant* Interviews can be stressful situations which may cause you to perspire more, so be prepared.
- *Shoes* These should be polished, in a dark rather than a bright colour. Don't wear spike heels and make sure if the shoes are high that you can walk without falling over.
- *Hair* Should be clean, neat, and tied back, if long. No wild colours, please — though DTPs, designers and illustrators often tend to look more funky, but it is usually safer to err on the side of caution.
- *Clothing* Should be clean, ironed, with no holes, and must be appropriate for the job, so if you are applying for a job in the warehouse you may choose to dress differently from how you would if you were applying for a job in production or reception.
- *Don't wear* cartoon socks or ties, panty hose with ladders, strong aftershave or perfume, visible body piercing other than the ears, bare midriff or décolleté, or tight clothing.

'Presenting well at interview and applying for jobs are skills that can be learnt and people do get better with practice. It's never the end of the world if you don't get a particular job and keeping that in mind will help you to relax, particularly at the interview. Being prepared is the other critical thing that will help you to feel comfortable. As far as possible try and look on the process as a meeting where your objective is to convey how suitable you are for the job. Have an agenda — three or four things you are going to get across during the course of the interview. Plan answers to questions you think you may be asked and rehearse them. It is very difficult to overprepare.'

Susan Ainsworth, HR Consultant and Lecturer in Management and Human Resources, RMIT

10 Career advice

What follows in this chapter are quotes from those in the book trade in response to questions I posed in a questionnaire. Their answers give valuable insights into how to succeed. Let them be an inspiration to you.

The best career advice

What was the most valuable piece of career advice anyone ever gave you?

'My father always told me that if I wanted to do it, then I could!'
Patricia Genat, Head of Division, ACER

'Set your goals and go for it!'
Rina Afflitto, Executive Director, Australian Booksellers Association

'If you want to make a lot of money, don't go into publishing.'
Tony Davies, Deputy Director, Cambridge University Press

'Keep your mouth shut, eyes and ears open and work hard!'
Mersina Malakellis, Key Accounts Manager, Random House

'Don't panic! The second best piece of information was to read the *Weekly Book Newsletter*. A private subscription is, unfortunately, expensive, but it carries news of the book trade, upcoming courses, and positions vacant.'
Carolyn Leslie, Editor, Non-fiction, HarperCollins

'Write what you would like to read.'
Jane Routley, Freelance Writer, author of Mage Heart

'Don't give up! The publishing industry is notoriously difficult to break into and it can get pretty disheartening being told that you can't get into it unless you have some publishing experience. (The old Catch-22!) I had a few encouraging mentors who told me to keep trying and that eventually I'd get in. And I did!'
Michelle Atkins, Copyright and Permissions Editor/Contracts Controller/Primary Editor, Nelson ITP

'A friend who persuaded me to enrol in the MBA program told me that I would only be satisfied when I was working for myself, for my own company.'
Barbara Cullen, General Manager and Director, Page One

'Use the opportunities presented and always be willing to push yourself beyond your comfort zone!'
Jo Breese, CEO, Booksellers New Zealand

'Well, actually, nobody has ever given me advice that relates to my overall career. People have, from time to time, made suggestions about the structure of my CV, but that's about as far as it's gone. It's more a case of taking opportunities as they arise and asking people for advice at the time. I've learnt that things change very quickly in this industry!'
Andrew Watson, Assistant Director, Melbourne University Press

'Never take no for an answer.'
Christine Farmer, National Publicity Manager, HarperCollins

'It's not what you know, it's who you know.'
Tamara Briggs, Receptionist, Blackwell Science Asia

'Scrub up well at the interview and you should get the job even if you're not the most qualified or experienced candidate; also, "never assume anything" (Rule Number 1 of editing!).'
Deborah Doyle, Freelance Book Editor and Teacher

'My Dad said, "Stick at it, kid!"'
Kristen Baragwanath, Acquisitions Editor, Schools Division, McGraw-Hill

'Don't expect it to be easy.'
Michelle Phillips, Publishing Assistant, ACER

'Enjoy your work or find another job.'
Ernie Tucker, Freelance Children's Literature Consultant/Acting Manager, St Martin's Youth Initiative Program

'In your career, current job and the business you work in, learn to love change. Endeavour to identify where change is required, participate in it until it is successful and then go find other areas that need improving.'
Ron Caithness, Operations Manager, Penguin Books Australia

'Do something you love. The rest follows.'
Helen Elliott, Literary Editor, Herald-Sun

'It's who you know not what you know!'
Louis de Vries, Manager, AGPS Victoria

'Read out aloud to yourself what you have just written.'
Sid Cowling, Author

'Don't burn your bridges — always leave on good terms with your employer.'
Paula Barrios, Design and Production Assistant, Reed Education

'Mum told me never to change my plans for a man (and Michael, my fellow director's dad told him "When in doubt, look helpless")!'
Stephanie Johnston, Director, Wakefield Press

'Get out of the office!'
Peter Donoughue, Manager Director, Jacaranda Wiley

'Trust no-one and improve your grammar!'
Jeremy Fisher, General Manager, Tertiary Division, McGraw-Hill

'Mistakes are inevitable, what is critical is how you manage them.'
Ray Coffey, Publisher, Fremantle Arts Centre Press

'Always be nice to everyone in publishing, you never know when you might be working for them.'
Susan Hawthorne, Publisher/Director, Spinifex Press

'Don't give up if you really want something, keep striving for it.'
Belinda Bolliger, Children's Publisher, Hodder Headline

'Treat the business as if it were your own.'
Lucie Pepeyan, Manager, General Book Department, McGills

'Be an active listener. This is the surest way to achieving customer satisfaction and be patient.'
Peter Milne, Deputy Managing Director, Abbey's Bookshops

'Get to know your books, get to know your customers, and put the two together. Product and customer knowledge is invaluable.'
Ian Tucker, General Manager, STMP Division, Harcourt Brace & Co.

'Get moving (in the sense of achieving the next step in your career) — there are lots of qualified youngsters coming up who want your job.'
Abigail Freeman, HR Manager, Addison Wesley Longman

'Work has to be fun and enjoyable. If you're not having fun look for something else.'
Benny Belbin, Sales and Marketing Manager, Capricorn Link

'If you want a certain career badly enough and you are willing to work for it, then eventually you will succeed.'
Melinda Bufton, Marketing Assistant, Bookstaff

Advice for an entry-level position

'Be sure to have gained at least some experience through work experience, volunteer, or a casual position in publishing or a related industry. Employers are often faced with a host of equal-ranking applicants for jobs and you must have something that marks you out as more suitable than the next person.'
Andrew Watson, Assistant Director, Melbourne University Press

'To read as much as they can: newspapers, magazines, medal winners and escapist stuff. To only stay in a job where they are having fun and learning something.'
Patricia Genat, Head of Division, ACER

'Mark Macleod (Children's Publishing Director) once told me, "Don't be afraid to lose your darlings". He was referring to

an author's favourite lines in a manuscript. If something doesn't work, it doesn't work, no matter how clever the line. Thanks to Mark's advice I learned very early not to be too precious with my work. The fact that Andrew Bennetto employed me primarily because I took the initiative to seek employment at LBC Information Services rather than respond to a position that became available, taught me a lot about pursuing goals rather than waiting around hoping that something would come up.'
John Larkin, Programmer/Analyst, LBC Information Services and Author

'Project your personality as a bright and good person so that employers will want to employ you. You must have some computer skills, of course, and be able to speak and think (and write) clearly — but personality is the key.'
Tony Davies, Deputy Director, Cambridge University Press

'Seek out any opportunity to work with books, even if your first job may not be what you want to do for the rest of your life. Look for the short-term opportunities as well as the long-term ones, at least they will give you some contacts. Work on your computer skills — with each passing day more work is done on computer. Show people that you are keen to keep on learning — take short courses, develop your skills in the things that you are passionate about. And read — keep up with what is available in the bookstores and show that you are aware of ideas that are being debated in the book world.'
Carolyn Leslie, Editor, Non-fiction, HarperCollins

'Be persistent. Remember Steven Donaldson [bestselling American science fiction author] had his book rejected by every publisher in the US, and the list of other writers with enormous numbers of rejections is long and illustrious.'
Jane Routley, Author of Mage Heart

'Be prepared to do anything (not in the Melrose Place sense!), even voluntary work. Any exposure (ditto Melrose gag) is going to help you gain a greater insight into an industry that can be a bit elusive to the outsider.'
Michelle Atkins, Copyright and Permissions Editor/Contracts Controller/Primary Editor, Nelson ITP

'Be persistent (but nicely) — do tertiary courses to gain knowl-

edge, find expertise and advice from industry people and talk to booksellers.'
Barbara Cullen, General Manager and Director, Page One

'Accept any job to get a foot in the door. Volunteering can be a good place to start and become known. If you are doing a course, check on its acceptance by the industry before committing time and money.'
Jo Breese, CEO, Booksellers New Zealand

'Do a lot of research about the industry you want to get into, and show initiative and enthusiasm.'
Rina Afflitto, Executive Director, Australian Booksellers Association

'We have to direct people looking for advice on how to get into publishing, because quite a few have quite unrealistic expectations, and I think that's where some of the courses around are going to be quite helpful for them. Even if they just look at the subjects offered in those courses. Even if they don't take the initiative and do the courses.'
Susan Blackwell, Executive Director, Australian Publishers Association

'Get the qualifications required for the job and promote your love of books. Be positive and upbeat and research the type of company you are applying for as there are many different styles of publisher.'
Christine Farmer, National Publicity Manager, HarperCollins

'Start at the bottom, ask for work experience, take a short course, always show initiative.'
Tamara Briggs, Receptionist, Blackwell Science Asia

'Do some intensive grammar, construction and punctuation classes to maximise your verbal and written communication skills. Do an editing course, read widely and have an idea of where you want your career to go — have a five-year plan'.
Deborah Doyle, Freelance Editor and Lecturer

'I would recommend persistence as a big factor in breaking into publishing (I got knocked back twice from the Graduate Diploma at RMIT). Building up skills and contacts should also be high on the list of priorities. If you're not interested in any

of that advice, I'd suggest getting in touch with Alison. It will be like a tonic for your career!'
Kristen Baragwanath, Acquisitions Editor, Schools Division, McGraw-Hill

'Research the job thoroughly. Don't be afraid to phone up strangers and ask. This initiative often impresses. Be there, for example, at book launches, events, bookshops. For a publisher, know the stock and what's coming up. Have opinions about what you like to read.'
Ernie Tucker, Freelance Children's Literature Consultant, Acting Manager, St Martin's Youth Initiative Program

'After obtaining their highest possible qualification, network within the industry, being prepared to take both lower level positions as well as a wider range of jobs.'
Ron Caithness, Operations Manager, Penguin Books Australia

'Talk to as many people as you can in the industry — don't be scared to ring or write to people you don't know, because somebody will hold the answer. While you are doing this enrol in relevant courses and work on gaining as many computer skills as you can.'
Michelle Phillips, Publishing Assistant, ACER

'Be persistent. But not overconfident about your own abilities.'
Helen Elliott, Literary Editor, Herald-Sun

'Never give up, keep on trying, start at the bottom.'
Louis de Vries, Manager AGPS Victoria

'Gain as wide experience as you can in all aspects of a profession to help you decide which aspects interest you the most.'
Sid Cowling, Author

'Ask for work experience and try to get your foot in the door that way. Persevere and take any task you are asked to do seriously. Be as efficient as you can be and demonstrate initiative.'
Paula Barrios, Design and Production Assistant, Reed Education

'Keep an open mind and stay enthusiastic.'
David Gaunt, Co-Proprietor, Gleebooks

'Start reading. Work in bookshops for a period of time.

Determine which area/s you are aiming at: Bookselling, Finance, Information Technology, Human Resources, Publishing, Distribution, Freight etc.'
Dennis Jones, Director, Dennis Jones & Associates

'Be prepared to accept anything which will lead you onto the right job. Be prepared to work hard and show *initiative*.'
Belinda Bolliger, Children's Publisher, Hodder Headline

'Get some hands-on experience, of any kind, in a publishing house. Once in, try a few different positions so you understand what happens in other areas. Be well-read.'
Susan Hawthorne, Publisher/Director, Spinifex Press

'Enthusiasm will get you everywhere, as well as an interest in publishing and books as a *career*.'
Production Manager

'As a translator, such positions don't really exist in Australia, freelancing is the only option. Don't expect it to be easy, but if you've got the perseverance and determination, go for it!'
Freelance Translator

'Be prepared for the ups and downs of your career. Make sure it's what you want to do — always think laterally!'
Michael Holman, Manager, Southbank Book

'Even if you want to get into publishing get some experience in a bookshop so you will understand the impact of the decisions that you may eventually make. If you are looking for a fascinating, compulsive industry where one day is never the same as the last with a fascinating product, try the book industry — you will probably never be rich but you will never be bored.'
Jean Ferguson, Book Industry Consultant

'Grab anything — getting your foot in the door is what counts — then it's entirely up to you! It worked for me! Also, don't be afraid to get your hands dirty, learn as much as you can and try and understand all the processes involved!'
Sales and Marketing Director

'Begin in Sales and Marketing. View all areas of the industry before you decide which you most like.'
Sales and Marketing Director

'Get work experience — write a letter offering to do any tasks, however menial, and do them cheerfully and well!'
Stephanie Johnston, Director, Wakefield Press

'Knock on doors and get advice from people who are already working in the area of publishing you aspire to. Try and get yourself a mentor: that way you don't have to reinvent the wheel.

'As for being a published writer, there are no short cuts. You have to be prepared to work hard and write every spare moment you get and have shoulders that are broad enough to carry the weight of setbacks. It is often quoted that approximately 99% of manuscripts are rejected. You simply have to be doing it better than the other 99%. This doesn't mean having cutting edge technology on which you produce your work; or graphically designed cover titles. Nor does it mean dotting your i's with hearts and little smiley faces. It is the content of your work that is all-important.'
John Larkin, Programmer/Analyst, LBC Information Services and Author

'Apply for a sales job. The knowledge you get is absolutely invaluable and you can go anywhere from there.'
Peter Donoughue, Managing Director, Jacaranda Wiley Ltd.

'Try to keep in mind that everybody has to start somewhere, and not everybody in more senior positions is completely stupid and incompetent (though some are).'
Jeremy Fisher, General Manager, Tertiary Division, McGraw-Hill

'Talk to people in various areas of the industry so that you can ascertain what career path you are looking for. Once you have made those initial contacts, try to secure some unpaid work experience — it may lead to a paid position and if it doesn't, it gives you essential exposure to the industry. This is how I started!'
Melinda Bufton, Marketing Assistant, Bookstaff

Advice for someone from a different profession

'Good people and managerial skills, and project management in particular, should be easily transferred. Being a good reader helps! Having a keen eye for an opportunity and the bottom line certainly helps.'
Patricia Genat, Head of Division, ACER

'Be prepared to work for less money.'
Tony Davies, Deputy Director, Cambridge University Press

'Look at the skills you have, and see how they would fit in with the book trade, and be passionate and committed about making the change.'
Carolyn Leslie, Editor, Non-fiction, HarperCollins

'Follow your dreams. Life is no good without them.'
Jane Routley, Freelance Writer and Author of Mage Heart

'Go for it! The book trade is worth the move! Make sure that you highlight all your transferable skills in your CV and accumulate as much related experience as your can (for example, do book reviews, go to any relevant short courses and try and chat to people in the industry for tips).'
Michelle Atkins, Copyright and Permissions Editor/Contracts Controller/Primary Editor, Nelson ITP

'Be certain. Find out what costs are involved before you give up a lucrative career.'
Barbara Cullen, General Manager and Director, Page One

'Become a volunteer, get a foot in the door somewhere. Sell the transferability of your skills.'
Jo Breese, CEO, Booksellers New Zealand

'I would have to question the motives of a mature-age move into publishing. In my experience, such people usually want to be writers! However, I have known people from other professions (especially legal and teaching) who have been successful but they are few and far between.'
Andrew Watson, Assistant Director, Melbourne University Press

'Work out what qualifications you have that are suitable for that position in the book trade and then work out how to enhance them. When I joined William Collins many staff objected as I was not "book trained". Now people only know me because of "books".'
Christine Farmer, National Publicity Manager, HarperCollins

'Do your research and talk to the relevant professional organisations.'
Rina Afflitto, Executive Director, Australian Booksellers Association

'Why do you want to work in the area? If you can't answer this clearly, speak to people in the industry in order to crystallise your career plan, then put it into action!'
Melinda Bufton, Marketing Assistant, Bookstaff

'Do as many courses as possible that cover specific aspects of the trade, but work out what your main strengths are: what specific skills can you bring to the position you're interested in? Compile a professional-looking CV and join professional associations to make contacts.'
Deborah Doyle, Freelance Editor and Lecturer

'Identify the skills and qualities which you can bring to the book trade, and focus on those when marketing yourself.'
Kristen Baragwanath, Acquisitions Editor, Schools Division, McGraw-Hill

'Do some book trade short courses, network; discuss career opportunities with recruitment agencies/ larger publishers and bookshops — then network again.'
Ron Caithness, Operations Manager, Penguin Books Australia

'Think about what skills you are presently using and how they could be transferable. Work on filling any gaps.'
Michelle Phillips, Publishing Assistant, ACER

'Find out what training or education is needed to move into the specific area and go from there.'
Paula Barrios, Design and Production Assistant, Reed Education and Professional Publishing

'Network, network and prove you can write or speak in public if these are important for that position.'
Ernie Tucker, Freelance Children's Literature Consultant

'Ask for work experience, take a short course.'
Tamara Briggs, Receptionist, Blackwell Science Asia

'Be prepared to work for less money, be polite in the face of adversity, don't give up trying for positions that appear to be of interest and learn to spell.'
Jeremy Fisher, General Manager, Tertiary Division, McGraw-Hill

'Apply for a sales job — if you're any good, you'll be noticed.'
Peter Donoughue, Managing Director, Jacaranda Wiley

'Think twice!'
Stephanie Johnston, Director, Wakefield Press

'Write and send CV to major publishers directed to the appropriate person. Keep an eye on the *Weekly Book Newsletter*, network the industry.'
Sales and Marketing Director

One piece of advice about breaking in

'I'm not sure whether people do "break in"? Somehow it just seems a natural place to be. Booksellers and publishers match words to people. If you think you'd be good at that — you're in!'
Patricia Genat, Head of Division, ACER

'Be persistent.'
Tony Davies, Deputy Director, Cambridge University Press

'Make sure where you work is where you wish to spend a lot of your life. Will you be happy with your work mates? Are there enough challenges there for your particular career path?'
Kevin Parken, Managing Director, Book Agencies of Adelaide

'Make sure that you really do want to work with books — loads of people want to work in the industry, but the money's not terrific and the pressures can be tough. If you still want to do this, then look for every opportunity to work with books and then around book people.'
Carolyn Leslie, Editor, Non-fiction, HarperCollins

'I know it's incredibly unoriginal, but here goes: Don't give up! Genuine passion to be a part of the industry will be appreciated by an interviewer one of these days.'
Michelle Atkins, Copyright and Permissions Editor/Contracts Controller/Primary Editor, Nelson ITP

'Don't give up. Talk to people in the industry.'
Barbara Cullen, General Manager and Director, Page One

'Keep trying — it is not easy to break in so be innovative in your approaches and get to know the people.'
Jo Breese, CEO, Booksellers New Zealand

'Find some way to undertake work experience or casual work first. It is always better to be a "known quantity" than a risk

when a potential employer is considering your application. And, sometimes, casual workers can become indispensable!'
Andrew Watson, Assistant Director, Melbourne University Press

'Giving advice to people on how to enter the industry — I try to find out what they're interested in, and where their interest lies, and what they've done in the past, and how that might assist them in getting a job in a particular firm. Then, tell them very quickly what the pay rates are, because that will really focus their minds. Many of them have a romantic notion about the industry, even after you've tried to dissuade them. They tend to think that it's all cocktail parties, authors and overseas book fairs. It's not! So you see, I'll talk to them about where their interests lie and, depending on their qualifications and what they've studied, I'll tell them about the Macquarie and Macleay courses in Sydney. If they're from Melbourne, I'll talk to them about the RMIT and Monash and other courses around, and Writers' Centres, if they're interested in that sort of activity. This can often fulfil a very useful role, particularly for would-be writers. Getting into the community of publishing — they can join Women in Publishing, they can join the Society of Editors and the Galley Club — so there's a strong networking bond that already exists for them to get in and meet people. They're not going to get in, probably, on their first job application. They should keep an eye on the arts pages of the *Sydney Morning Herald* for jobs, and in the positions vacant in the classifieds of the *Herald* and the *Age* and other newspapers around the country, although the bulk of publishing is located in Sydney and Melbourne. Increasingly, there are opportunities in Brisbane, and interestingly, Perth too. So it's not just confined to the eastern seaboard. So you try and head them in the right direction, whilst also giving them a realistic view of just how challenging it can be. You try to encourage them to think about sales and marketing, not just editorial work. Not everybody is suited to that incredible detail required in editorial work. I personally think that marketing is a very stimulating area — you get to work on every title across the board, where editors only work on a selection of titles, perhaps in their subject range. Marketing, I think, can often be a very exciting area. Publicity and promotion, too, can really get you out among a lot more people. Women in particular have done extremely well across all these areas. Publishing is an industry in which

women can do very well — sales, marketing, production, design, editing — all facets have been very attractive and very conducive to women.'
Susan Blackwell, Executive Director, Australian Publishers' Association

'Don't go in with grandiose ideas. Remember to be commercial and think about "what will sell". (Sneak in some grandiose ideas about books that will change the world later, when you have a proven track record!)'
Christine Farmer, National Publicity Manager, HarperCollins

'Don't do it for the money. Do it for personal satisfaction — you'll be creating something from nothing. The pay is generally low. The trade seems glamorous but the work is actually 90 per cent perspiration — you have to be content to be in crisis mode most of the time.'
Deborah Doyle, Freelance Editor and Lecturer

'Stick at it!'
Kristen Baragwanath, Acquisitions Editor, Schools Division, McGraw-Hill

'Network to create opportunities, preparing for interviews before you have them. If you get a "break" work hard at it.'
Ron Caithness, Operations Manager, Penguin Books Australia

'Find out as much as you can about the industry — this will help you break in and also to work out whether it is the field for you.'
Michelle Phillips, Publishing Assistant, ACER

'Only do it if you love it — there's no money!'
Helen Elliott, Literary Editor, Herald-Sun

'Don't look to get rich.'
Louis de Vries, Manager, AGPS Victoria

'Do it!'
Sid Cowling, Author

'Persevere.'
Paula Barrios, Design and Production Assistant, Reed Education and Professional Publishing

'Call back after the interview to see how the decision making

process is progressing — shows you are really interested in the
job. Don't be a 9 to 5 person.'
Production Manager

'Always offer to special order anything!'
David Gaunt, Co-proprietor, Gleebooks

'Work out what skills you can bring to the job or company
that no one else can — then make sure you communicate this
in the interview.'
HR Manager

'It sounds old fashioned, but it is timeless: Be positive, terribly
careful, and ever ready to roll up your sleeves and see a task
right through — always! A fair-minded boss will give you a
break soon enough.'
*Nick Walker, Director, Australian Scholarly Publishing and
Lecturer in Charge, Graduate Diploma in Publishing & Editing,
Monash University*

'Get out there and network. Also, be pro-active about getting
your name in front of as many people as possible, any way
you can. If you are a marketing person responsible for direct
mail, make sure that you send your direct marketing pieces to
every marketing manager in the industry — and do it in a
subtle way by simply adding the names on to the back of a
regular mailing. Don't send a covering letter announcing how
fantastic you are 'as can be judged by these superb examples'.
If you want a particular job, make sure that the people who
make the decisions know of you. Those people trying to get
in for the first time should take whatever they can get. It's a
small industry and you get a lot of people saying "I want to
be an editor", but even if you've gone through a course and
got the relevant qualification, take what you can get as a
starting point and then move towards your goal. Some people
will take the high moral ground and say, "If I'm not going to
be offered a job as an editor, then I'm not going to do it". To
me, that's crazy. They have to get real and say I've got to get
down from there and be a secretary, a receptionist, a sales
person, a store person whatever. It won't do them any harm
and eventually they will be able to move into that editorial
stream, for sure. You have to get into the industry any way
you can and once you're in, you can move around. The

industry is fantastically networked, so once you are in through
the door, the biggest obstacle is out of the way.'
Robert Coco, Publisher, Pearson Professional

11 Courses available

'There are numerous external courses that are useless and not accredited. Be very careful selecting courses and ask advice. Seek industry-based courses and always attend courses offered by your employer even if it means giving up your free time.'
Jean Ferguson, Book Industry Consultant

'I really enjoy what I do, and so talking to other people about it — as a guest lecturer in several publishing courses — does not seem like work at all.'
Susan Keogh, Senior Editor, Melbourne University Press

'Look for the most applicable course and apply yourself.'
Ian Tucker, General Manager, STMP Division, Harcourt Brace & Co.

'Swinburne University has some excellent courses on innovation and opportunity and should be included in your educational mix.'
Dennis Jones, Director, Dennis Jones & Associates

'I think everyone should attend a retail booksellers' course — that's one of the most fundamental parts of our business.'
Benny Belbin, Sales & Marketing Manager, Capricorn Link

'The RMIT course is excellent for a broad overview of publishing with particular emphasis on editorial.'
Paula Hurley, Educational Sales & Marketing Manager, Penguin Books Australia

'Don't get sucked into thinking publishing is just about editing. Most publishing certificates or diplomas focus too heavily on that one aspect of the complex business.'
Peter Donoughue, Managing Director, Jacaranda Wiley

'Talk to others who have done the course to ensure it is reputable. Ask publishers/prospective employers if they think it is worthwhile doing.'
Stephanie Johnston, Director, Wakefield Press

'Select a course that is going to complement your experience or will demonstrate you are committed in a certain direction.'
Abigail Freeman, Human Resources Manager, Addison Wesley Longman

Industry advice

There are a myriad of courses available — the key issue is to find a course that best suits your interests, career plans, time and budget. Make sure that any course you undertake is recognised by the industry. Courses with editing, publishing, bookselling components and majors run by universities and TAFEs, and in particular through professional industry groups (such as the Society of Editors, the Australian Publishers Association, the Australian Booksellers Association and the Galley Club) are a good option. In New Zealand there is the Whitireia Community Polytechnic Certificate, the Local Publishers Forum, and the Bookselling Certificate offered by Booksellers New Zealand. An industry-approved or recognised course will be one that has a good response from potential employers.

Sometimes the most prestigious courses (such as the Macquarie University Graduate Diploma in Publishing and Editing and the RMIT Graduate Diploma in Publishing and Editing) limit their students to those working in the trade only. This means that out of the many hundreds who apply, only those who are currently working in publishing would have any real chance of gaining a place. This is because the course was originally set up to fill a need within the publishing profession, and so preference is still given to those who are working for a publisher. Some courses require two or more applications. One of my students applied three times before gaining entry to the RMIT course, however by the third time, she had a job in a publishing house, had undertaken some shorter courses and submitted an excellent application.

Some courses are full fee paying, whilst others, such as those that provide an industry overview, will probably be moderate in costs. It is wise to take on one of these courses before committing yourself to a more expensive undertaking. If however, you are 100% confident that this is the course for you, then go right ahead!

Talk to past and present students — they will be a good source of information about how the course actually matches up to the brochure or industry gossip. Talk (and then listen!) to potential employers — publishers and industry bodies and get their opinion. The courses will take time, energy and effort, so you have to be sure before you commit yourself that it will benefit your career.

If you are unsure about which area of publishing you wish to head for, a short or introductory course can work wonders! I have taught many students who thought that they wanted to be an editor until they went through an intense session, and found out that the reality was not what they thought! Don't be blind to the many other jobs out there, and take on every opportunity to visit open days and get as clear an understanding as you can about the course and the educational/trade body behind it. Beware of advertisements for courses that promise or guarantee work.

What the lecturers and industry say . . .

'The Design & Desktop Publishing course is of approximately 600 hours duration and covers a wide range of subject areas and so provides broad-based training for DTP and graphic designers. The content ranges from introduction for computers for graphic arts, software applications, basic design, typography and printing processes. Students will go on to more advanced training or move directly into the industry as a self-employed DTP or work for a trade house, printer or advertising agency.'
John Bright, Program Manager, Department of Applied Design, Hobart Institute of TAFE

'We offer a single subject called "Editing and Publishing" which is a part of our major in Public Relations and Journalism. Therefore, students studying these courses can do this subject as an interest elective. The subjects the elective covers

include basic sub-editing and editing skills, the history of printing and printing processes, as well as ethical and legal issues which affect publishers, such as defamation and copyright. There is also a strong focus on typography and design. This is very much a "hands on" course where students learn DTP and web publishing skills and have to create their own publications as a part of the subject.'
Associate Professor Mark Pearson, Head of Communication and Media Studies, Bond University

'Our course (Professional Writing and Editing: Certificate IV/Diploma of Arts) offers students the opportunity to study writing in an adult environment with highly professional tutors who are all writers. Our central city locality and flexible daytime and evening timetable enable quick access for students who are employed during the day. One core module, "Industry Overview", is offered at a Summer School in January, enabling students to attain a grasp of the writing and publishing profession before commencing their specific studies.'
Mary Manning, Coordinator Professional Writing and Editing, Council of Adult Education

'I recommend the CAE course "Become a Bookseller".'
Rina Afflitto, Executive Director, ABA

'Obviously, I would encourage the new bookseller to undertake the Certificate of Bookshop Practice run by the ABA, attend the annual conference and any ABA seminars in their region.'
Jean Ferguson, Book Industry Consultant

'Get advice from publishers or one of the industry trade groups first to ensure it is a recognised course.'
John Larkin, Programmer/Analyst, Law Book Company

'Do it! It's helping develop your skills even if you end up a missionary in deepest darkest Africa, it may come in handy knowing how to handle that last comma!'
Kristen Baragwanath, Acquisitions Editor, Schools Division, McGraw-Hill

'Check it (the course) out very carefully. Look at who is teaching the course, find out what material will be covered, and what skills you can expect to have achieved by the end of the course. Perhaps make a call to a body like the Society

of Editors to see if the course is one that they know of and (perhaps) recommend.'
Carolyn Leslie, Editor, Non-fiction, HarperCollins

'I'd recommend the ABA Certificate of Bookshop Practice.'
Kevin Parken, Managing Director, Book Agencies of Adelaide

'My recommendation is for the Graduate Diploma in Editing and Publishing at Macquarie University and the Macleay College course (with research about the costs).'
Jeremy Fisher, General Manager, Tertiary Division, McGraw-Hill

'Choose carefully. Not all courses lead to jobs and there is an oversupply of [course] places compared to jobs available. The course itself must be suitable for the kind of job you want — does it concentrate on editing, production or just give an industry overview?'
Andrew Watson, Deputy Director, Melbourne University Press

'Everyday I find myself drawing on the skills I acquired while studying for the Graduate Diploma in Editing and Publishing at RMIT. Everything the course gave me has proven invaluable for my career: the skills, the knowledge, the contacts, and most importantly, the appreciation of a fine bottle of red — thanks, Professor Curtain!'
Caroline Birrell, Editor, Weekly Book News; *Assistant Editor,* Australian Bookseller & Publisher

'Start somewhere by listing your skills and personal characteristics which will help you decide what subjects to take. Try to get into as many courses as possible and if at first you don't succeed, try, try again.'
Deborah Doyle, Lecturer, RMIT Professional Writing and Editing

'The course is designed to provide students with an overview of the publishing industry in Australia today, and to give them practical skills to enter the industry in either editing, production management or marketing. They also gain an understanding of the importance of the book as a cultural object.'
John Arnold, Deputy Director of the National Centre for Australian Studies, Course Co-ordinator Graduate Diploma in Publishing & Editing, Monash University

'The type of person who does my courses tends either to

embrace the idea of working with books and leaps headfirst into further, more focused study or a book-related job, or they tend to decide that the work is not of interest and go and do something completely different.'
Alison Aprhys, Lecturer 'Introduction to Book Publishing',
'Careers in the Book Trade' and 'Become a Bookseller'

'I recommend the ABA Certificate of Bookshop Practice.'
Peter Milne, Deputy Managing Director, Abbey's Bookshops

'Macleay College has a good all-round basic course.'
Sally Stokes, Production Manager, Lansdowne
Publishing/Macquarie Dictionary

What the students say . . .

'I'm interested in all aspects of book, magazine and multi-media publishing. This course has opened many doors for me, such as undertaking unpaid work experience with a publishing consultant; opportunities to make contacts in the industry and explore all the different areas of the profession that I didn't know existed. This is important as it means that I'm not limiting my career opportunities. It's good to be able to keep up with what is happening on the cutting edge in the industry as well as having a solid foundation of the publishing back-ground. You are made aware of the professional organisations you can join, and seminars you can attend that are directly related to the course content, allowing them to be put in to a practical context. The course exposes you to professionals in the industry who are experts in their field. They give guest lectures and keep us informed of the latest publishing devel-opments.'
Sascha Jeske, Student, Graduate Diploma in Publishing &
Editing, Monash University

'After deciding that I wanted to do this course I applied through the university and was eventually granted an interview in late November. At this stage I had to think hard why I wanted to enrol in the course because I knew that would be one of the questions asked. I knew that I wanted to be an editor and I thought that I had the necessary attributes to be one. In the interview I stated clearly why I wanted to do the course, reassuring the selection committee that I was keen to work in the industry and so give this new course a good name.

I found out before Christmas that I had been accepted and then tackled the problem of finding the money to pay my up-front fees. The National Australia Bank was good enough to give me a student loan which I don't have to pay back for five years. Without this assistance I don't think I would have been able to consider it. I suppose the most important question is how will this course help me find a job in the industry? I can only look at this from a potential employers' position and my research shows that it's regarded favourably.'
Morgan Mahony, Student, Graduate Diploma Publishing &
Editing, Monash University

I feel I am fortunate to be balancing the theory of the publishing course with a part-time job at Melbourne University Press. I'm undertaking general administrative work including permissions, relief reception, keyboarding, correspondence and answering calls. It's a marvellous opportunity to get the big picture on how this publishing house works within the book industry.'
Jo Lamborn, Publishing Student and Publishing Assistant,
Melbourne University Press

List of publishing courses

Name & type/duration	Institution	Content	Selection criteria	Fees	Closing dates	Contact details
Professional Writing & Editing (Diploma)	RMIT, TAFE	* Editing, *Professional writing, * Writer and research, * Practical placement, * IT (Word-processing), * Desktop publishing, * Industry overview, * Design and production, * Non-fiction, * Short story, * Novel, * Poetry, * Performance writing, * Screen-writing	* Year 12, * Mature age with evidence of ability or relevant industry experience, * Small number of places for Equal Opportunity students, * Accepts overseas and full fee-paying students	FT $551; PT $50–$410	FT 16/9; PT 28/10; mid-year places offered	Dept of English & Communication (03.9660 4261; 03.9660 4262)
Proofreading & Editing (short course)	Management Technology Education	* Proofreading; * Editing; *What to do when style books differ		$648; $550 group fee	24/7	Gail Burgess (03.9261 5555)

Name & type/ duration	Institution	Content	Selection criteria	Fees	Closing dates	Contact details
Introduction to Authoring Tools (short course)	APA	* Multi-media authoring		$75 (members); $95	23/8	APA (02.9281 9788)
Introduction to Book Publishing (short course)	Methodist Ladies College	* Book production, * Impact of changing technology, * Marketing, sales and distribution, * Copyright, * Careers, * Industry visit		$175		(03.9274 6412; 03.9274 6413)
Careers in Publishing (2-day seminar)	MLC	* Overview of publishing house, * Industry visit, * Impact of technology, * Editing process		$195		(03.9274 6412; 03.9274 6413)

Name & type/ duration	Institution	Content	Selection criteria	Fees	Closing dates	Contact details
Bookbinding and Finishing, initial trade course (3 years PT)	RMIT	* Binding, * Collating, * Finishing, * Case book manufacture, * Trimming, * Folding, * Section sewing, * Science and technology, * Communication, *Specialist streams:* * Machine processes, * Craft binding, * Specialist technology	Applicants must be registered apprentices in the trade. The RMIT brochure entitled 'General Information on Courses' is updated annually and outlines further entrance requirements	In 1996, fees were calculated at $1.14 per standard contact hour. Exact fees can only be calculated at the time of enrolment	Contact RMIT	RMIT Dept of Printing Machining and Finishing, Faculty of Art and Design (03.9389 9454)

Name & type/duration	Institution	Content	Selection criteria	Fees	Closing dates	Contact details
Graduate Certificate of Professional Writing/ Graduate Diploma of Professional Writing (Graduate certificate PT, 1–2 years; Graduate Diploma PT, 2–4 years)	Deakin University	* Editing, * Factual writing, * Fiction writing, * Script writing, * Poetry writing, * Writing for young children, * Writing for young adults, * Writing biography, * Writing local and family history (last four subject to approval)	Applicants for admission shall: * Hold an approved degree in a field other than those fields in professional writing or editing which those applicants are seeking to study; * Hold a qualification approved as equivalent to such a degree; or * Have satisfied special requirements for admission as determined from time to time. Applicants may be required to sit a written test	In 1997, all students undertaking either of the courses were charged tuition fees of $600 per credit point. Students are exempt from HECS but are required to pay the General Service Fee	30/11	Faculty Administration Officer, Faculty of Arts, Deakin University (03.9244 6378)

Name & type/ duration	Institution	Content	Selection criteria	Fees	Closing dates	Contact details
Certificate IV in Professional Writing and Editing (One year FT, or 3 or more years PT at day and evening classes)	CAE, Melbourne, city campus	* Construction of English, * Editing, * Industry overview, * Practical placement, * Non-fiction, * Short story, * Writer and research, * Poetry, * Performance writing, * Writing for children, * Novel, * Popular fiction, * Design and layout, * Information technology, * Literature analysis	Students are expected to have completed Year 12 (VCE) or its equivalent. Adult-entry students without Year 12 are required to demonstrate an appropriate standard of English and writing skills	TAFE fees and charges apply	13/12 for first-round offers; 13/1 for second-round offers and until course commences for any places remaining	Course Co-ordinator (03.9652 0638) or the Humanities Department (03.9652 0754)

Name & type/duration	Institution	Content	Selection criteria	Fees	Closing dates	Contact details
Graduate Diploma of Publishing and Editing (PT 2 years)	Griffith University	* Design principles and production systems, * Editing and project management, * Publishing cultures: history, law and ethics, * Publishing futures	Applicants will normally be expected to possess an appropriate undergraduate degree and, in addition, either industry experience or completion of a recognised copy-editing course. Basic word-processing skills are assumed	Fees are charged for subjects in the Graduate Diploma which does not attract HECS. The fee for Australian residents in 1997 is $1500 per subject. The total fee for the course is $6000. Student Administration fees will also be charged	Contact Department before December	Administration Officer (07.3875 7731)

Name & type/duration	Institution	Content	Selection criteria	Fees	Closing dates	Contact details
Printing Technology (FT 1 year; PT 2 years)	RMIT	Extensive course includes: * Workteam communications, * Introduction to computers, * Printing materials and applications, * Press techniques, * Fibreboard techniques, * Introduction to small business, * Environmental printing, * Post-press techniques	The course is offered to those working in the printing industry and also applicants who have satisfactorily completed an approved course of study at Year 12 level or equivalent. Consult current RMIT 'General Information on TAFE and Degree Courses' brochure for full requirements	In 1996, fees were calculated at $1.14 per standard contact hour. Exact fees can only be calculated at the time of enrolment	Contact RMIT	Department of Pre-Press and Screen Printing, Faculty of Art and Design (03.9389 9446)

Name & type/ duration	Institution	Content	Selection criteria	Fees	Closing dates	Contact details
RMIT Art, Design and Communication Faculty (Short courses: length varies between one session and several weeks, depending on the course)	RMIT	Courses are variable from semester to semester. These are examples of courses that have been offered in the past: * Introduction to book illustration, * Magazine editing and sub-editing, * Magazine publishing and production, * Introduction to multi-media, * Copy-editing and proofreading, * Media release writing, * Book binding techniques, * QuarkXPress for DTP	Most of the courses are open to anyone who is interested in the subject. Any entry requirements that may exist will be indicated	Vary according to course	Contact RMIT Short courses registration (03.9660 4100)	

Name & type/ duration	Institution	Content	Selection criteria	Fees	Closing dates	Contact details
Graduate Diploma in Editing and Publishing (PT 2 years)	RMIT	Subjects come under the following study areas: * Editing, * Production, * Cultural context, * Publishing/project management	Applicants must have a first degree from a recognised university and preference is given to applicants engaged in or with some experience in the area. As there is a high demand for places in the course, applicants are encouraged to add a short statement of their experience, interests and aspirations to the application	The course is only offered on a fee-paying basis. Contact Department for further details	Contact Department	Department of Communication Studies, Faculty of Social Sciences and Communications (03.9660 3146)

Name & type/ duration	Institution	Content	Selection criteria	Fees	Closing dates	Contact details
Bachelor of Communication/Diploma of Arts (Professional Writing and Editing). Double award (degree plus diploma) FT four years	Casey Institute of TAFE, Monash University	Subjects include: * Introduction to communication studies, * Media studies, * Non-fiction writing, * Practical placement, * Desktop publishing, * Corporate writing, * Content analysis and quantitative research	The general entrance requirement is satisfactory completion of the VCE or equivalent, with a grade average of D in units 3 and 4 of English	Contact Department for this information	Prospective students must apply through VTAC (03.9690 7977)	Monash University, Berwick Campus (03.9904 7111)

Name & type/ duration	Institution	Content	Selection criteria	Fees	Closing dates	Contact details
Careers in Publishing (*half-day seminar*)	Victorian Writers' Centre	Introduction to and overview of the career options available in the publishing industry	Open to Victorian Writers' Centre members, as well as interested public	The costs for attending seminar at the Centre vary, however a discount is always given to members	Contact the Centre for details	(03.9415 1077)

Name & type/ duration	Institution	Content	Selection criteria	Fees	Closing dates	Contact details
Design and Desktop Publishing Certificate (duration of course varies)	Hobart Institute of TAFE	Subjects include: * Introduction to computers for graphic arts, * Word-processing, * Desktop publishing, * Illustration, * Layout skills, * Basic design, * Writing workplace documents, * Printing processes	Basic keyboarding and word-processing skills are pre-requisites	Fees are variable. Contact Department	For closing date contact Department	Program Manager of Applied Design, Visual Arts, Crafts and Printing Section (03.6244 9432; 03.6244 9418)

Name & type/ duration	Institution	Content	Selection criteria	Fees	Closing dates	Contact details
Certificate of Bookshop Practice (3-part external course). There is also a CBP Fastrack course for members with over five years' experience	ABA	* Starting out, * Customer communication, * Sales techniques, * Consumer law, * Book knowledge, * Resources, * Communication with staff, * How a book is made, * Visual merchandising, * Copyright law, * Know your books, * Christian bookselling, * Financial management, * Bookselling and the law, * Book-buying skills, * Marketing, * Advertising, * Staff selection and training, * Computers in bookshops	Working in a bookshop	ABA members. Fee of $200 per stage for the first 2 stages. Stage 3 fee $300. Non-ABA members' fee $300 and $500 respectively. Fastrack CBP is for ABA members only, fee $595.	Call ABA	Call ABA (03.9663 7888)

Name & type/duration	Institution	Content	Selection criteria	Fees	Closing dates	Contact details
Diploma in Book Editing and Publishing (PT 16 weeks)	Macleay College, Sydney	* Editing manuscripts, * Book design, * Production process,* Publishing management	* Students currently sitting for HSC, * Graduates, * Mature-age	$2690	January and July	Macleay College (02.9360 2033)
Diploma of Arts, Professional Writing and Editing (FT 2 years; PT up to 8 years)	TAFE, Box Hill, Australian Academy of Vocational Arts	* Construction of English, * Industry overview, * Word processing, * 15 electives including small press publishing	* Folio of work, * Recent exercise, * Interview, * 19+ years old, or HSC equivalent	$1.00 per hour of tuition + $50	October	Secretary, Box Hill Institute (03.9286 9659); VTAC (03.9690 7977) for guidebook
Publishing Process and Principles of Editing (6 seminars)	NSW Writers' Centre	* Publisher, author and copyright, * Principles of editing, * Parts of a book, * Indexing and proofreading		$480; discounts for members	May and October	NSW Writers' Centre (02.9555 9757)

Name & type/ duration	Institution	Content	Selection criteria	Fees	Closing dates	Contact details
Practical Editing Workshops (2 days)	NSW Writers' Centre	Basic Editing		$140	July and November	NSW Writers' Centre (02.9555 9757)
Diploma in Editing and Publishing (PT 2 years)	Macquarie University	* Language, editing and writing I and II, * Design and Production, * Publishing and Management, * 2 options, * Practicum	* People involved in publishing industry or comparable, * Bachelor of Arts, 3-4 years' experience in publishing field	$206 per credit point; 24 credits	October	Associate Professor Peters (02.9850 8773); applications to the Registrar

Name & type/duration	Institution	Content	Selection criteria	Fees	Closing dates	Contact details
MA in Publishing, Coursework (FT 1 year; PT 2 years)	Monash University	* Culture and history of publishing industry, * Forms and developments in electronic publishing, * Principles and practice of management, * Development of analytical and writing skills in publishing research	* Persons of experience and standing in the industry, * Suitably qualified and experienced persons with cultural, political or management positions within the industry	$6600 HECS	October	National Centre for Australian Studies, Course Director, John Arnold (03.9905 9021)
MA in Publishing – Research (FT 1 year, PT 2 years)	Monash University	As above, plus: * Development of advanced conceptual skills for critical analysis of problems, * Cogent presentation of ideas, * Develop, plan and implement major research project	Professionals in the publishing industry	$6600 HECS	October	John Arnold (03.9905 9021)

Name & type/ duration	Institution	Content	Selection criteria	Fees	Closing dates	Contact details
Faculty Certificate in Publishing and Editing (6 months–1 year)	Monash University	* History of publishing and the impact of the book, * Authorship, editing and the text, * Electives: new convergent media or communications and media history or cultural policy	Either * Undergraduate degree or * Up to 3 years experience in publishing industry, * Communications or Public Affairs or personal publications	$3300	October	John Arnold (03.9905 9021)
Graduate Diploma of Arts, Publishing and Editing (FT one year, PT 18 months–2 years)	Monash University	First two above, and * Production processes, * New convergent media, * Publishing project, * Elective	* Undergraduate degree, * Interview for aptitude; is assisted by experience in the industry	$6600	October	John Arnold (03.9905 9021)

Name & type/ duration	Institution	Content	Selection criteria	Fees	Closing dates	Contact details
Graduate Diploma in Professional Writing (1 year)	Victoria University of Technology	* Writing as discourse, * Advanced editing and publishing, * Advanced screen-writing, * Magazine writing, * Popular fiction, * Principle of document design, * Technical writing for organisations, * Instructional writing, * Writing about science and technology, * Prose fiction, * Scripting, directing and producing the documentary, * Writing for PR and advertising, * Independent project	* Undergraduate degree or equivalent, * Demonstrated relevant professional background or experience that allows special admission, * Written selection exercise or samples of written work. NB Advanced standing up to one quarter of the course may be available	$3300 HECS	October	Michele Grossman, Senior Lecturer, Dept. Communication and Language Studies (03.9365 2247) or Associate Professor Helen Borland, Head of Department (03.9365 2247)

Name & type/ duration	Institution	Content	Selection criteria	Fees	Closing dates	Contact details
Whitireia Publishing Course	Whitireia Community Polytechnic/ Te Kura Matatin O Whitireia, New Zealand	* Editorial, * Production, * Trade knowledge and liaison, * Business management, * Personal development and management, * Portfolio	* Tertiary qualification and/or equivalent work or breadth of life experience, * Basic level of computer literacy, * Firm commitment to eventual work in the industry, * Interview for short-listed candidates. NB: Experience in publishing/book industry an advantage	$NZ3610–$NZ3964	November	Barbara Marshall, Whitireia Community Polytechnic (04.237 3100) or Daphne Brasell Associates (fax 04.237 3116)

NB: All information was correct at time of printing. Information may change from time to time.

Tertiary writing courses with editing components are offered by the following institutions:

- Bond University, School of Humanities, Ph (07) 5595 1111
- Box Hill Institute of TAFE, Ph (03) 9286 9659
- Casey Institute of TAFE, Monash University, Office of Prospective Students, Ph (03) 9905 1320/VTAC, Ph (03) 9690 7977
- Council of Adult Education, Victoria, Humanities Department, Ph (03) 9652 0754/Course Coordinator, Ph (03) 9652 0638
- Curtin University of Technology, Department of Communications and Cultural Studies, Ph (09) 351 2000
- Deakin University, Arts Faculty, Ph (03) 5227 2333/School of Literary and Communication Studies, Ph (03) 9244 5398
- Griffith University, Ph (07) 3875 5165
- James Cook University of Northern Queensland, Department of Modern Languages, Ph (077) 81 4111
- Macquarie University School of English, Linguistics and Media, Ph (02) 9850 7111
- Monash University, National Centre for Australian Studies, Ph (03) 9905 4000
- Royal Melbourne Institute of Technology, Department of English and Communication, Ph (03) 9660 4261/4262
- University of Newcastle, Department of Communication and Media Arts, Faculty of Arts and Social Sciences, Ph (049) 216 794
- University of Western Sydney, School of Humanities, Ph (045) 70 1333
- University of Wollongong, Ph (042) 213 867
- Victoria University of Technology, Ph (03) 9365 2247

12 Professional organisations

What follows is a listing of the general and special interest groups that abound for people in the book trade, or for those interested in becoming part of the book industry. There are three areas of special interest groups: general book trade interest groups, such as the Galley Club; specialist groups, such as the Australian Booksellers Association; and related groups, such as the Australian Medical Writers Association. Some of these organisations have strict and definite criteria for membership, others such as the National Book Council or Galley Club welcome nearly anyone with an interest in their aims and objectives. There is probably a group for every interest and profession!

Australia

Special interest group	Members
Association of University Presses	Recognised university publishers who are also members of the APA
Australian and New Zealand Association of Antiquarian Booksellers Limited PO Box 279 Cammeray NSW 2062 Ph: (02) 9331 1411 Fax: (02) 9361 3371	Antiquarian booksellers and booksellers engaged in the selling of old books of some worth or consequence

*Australian Book Designers'
Group*
12/11 Milton Street
Elwood Vic 3184
Ph/Fax: (03) 9531 5658

Book designers,
illustrators, DTP, graphic
designers, and production
staff

*Australian Booksellers
Association*
Suite 4, 21 Drummond Place
Carlton Vic 3053
(PO Box 1088
Carlton Vic 3053)
Ph: (03) 9663 7888
Fax: (03) 9663 7557

Booksellers: independent,
franchise, chain, would-be
bookshop owners and
suppliers of goods and
services to booksellers

*Australian Institute of
Interpreters*
Level 9, 300 Flinders Street
Melbourne Vic 3000
Ph: (03) 9614 1162
Fax: (03) 9629 4708

Interpreters and translators

*Australian Medical Writers'
Association*
PO Box 1261
Chatswood NSW 2067
Ph: 1 800 641 903

Medical journalists and
writers

*Australian Music Publishers
Association*
14th Floor, 56 Berry Street
North Sydney NSW 2060
(PO Box 2135
North Sydney NSW 2060)
Ph: (02) 9954 3655
Fax: (02) 9954 3664

Publishers and staff of
music periodicals, journals
and newsletters

*Australian Publishers
Association*
Suite 60/89 Jones Street
Ultimo NSW 2007
Ph: (02) 9281 9788
Fax: (02) 9281 1073

'Individuals, partnerships
or companies engaged in
the publishing of books,
scholarly journals,
educational material and
multi-media works as a

bona fide and continuing
operation'

Australian Society of Authors
96 Pitt Street
Redfern NSW 2016
(PO Box 1566
Strawberry Hills NSW 2012)
Ph: (02) 9318 0877
Fax: (02) 9318 0530

Published and unpublished
writers

Australian Society of Indexers
GPO Box 1251
Melbourne Vic 3000
Ph: (03) 9571 6341

Indexers and editors

*Canberra Guild of Craft
Bookbinders*
PO Box 4322
Kingston ACT 2604
Ph: (02) 6297 6117

Bookbinders

Children's Book Council
3 Woodridge Street
Moorooka Qld 4105

Booksellers, teachers,
librarians, students of
literature, publishing and
editorial students and
anyone interested in
children's books

*Christian Booksellers
Association*
Suite 2, 7–9 President Avenue
Caringbah NSW 2229
(PO Box 576
Caringbah NSW 2229)
Ph: (02) 9524 3347
Fax: (02) 9540 3001

Booksellers of Christian
literature and of
Australian material

*Fellowship of Australian
Writers*
State based. Check locally for
details

Writers

Galley Club
C/- Post Office 72
Port Melbourne Vic 3207
PO Box 983
Lane Cove NSW 2066

Book printers, editors, production staff, publishing and editorial students, sales reps and managers, marketing people and publishers

International Pen Melbourne
641 Inkerman Road
Caulfield North Vic 3161
(PO Box 143
Clifton Hill Vic 3068)
Ph: (03) 9690 9199
Fax: (03) 9663 8658

Writers

Media Entertainment and Arts Alliance
245 Chalmers Street
Redfern NSW 2016
(PO Box 723
Strawberry Hills NSW 2012)
Ph: (02) 9333 0999
Fax: (02) 9333 0933

Editors and journalists

National Book Council
Suite 3, 21 Drummond Place
Carlton Vic 3053
Ph: (03) 9663 8655
Fax: (03) 9663 8658

Booksellers, publishers, academics, students of literature, writers, authors and anyone interested in Australian books and writing

NSW Guild of Craft Bookbinders Inc
Writers Centre
Rozelle Hospital
Rozelle NSW 2039
Ph: (02) 9810 4974

Bookbinders

NSW Writers' Centre
PO Box 1056
Rozelle NSW 2039
Ph: (02) 9555 9757

Writers

Queensland Bookbinders   Bookbinders
Guild Inc
110 Andrew Avenue
Tarragindi Qld 4121
Ph: (07) 848 3774

Queensland Writers' Centre   Writers
PO Box 12059
Elizabeth Street
Brisbane Qld 4002
Ph: (07) 3839 1243

Society of Editors   Editors: freelance and
PO Box 176   in-house, publishing and
Carlton South Vic 3053   editorial students

PO Box 254
Broadway NSW 2007
Ph: (02) 9552 0039

PO Box 3222
Manuka ACT 2603

PO Box 1524
Toowong Qld 4066

PO Box 2328
Kent Town SA 5071

PO Box 32
Sandy Bay Tas 7055

SA Writers' Centre   Writers
187 Rundle Street
Adelaide SA 5000
(PO Box 43
Rundle Mall
Adelaide SA 5001)
Ph: (08) 8223 7662
Fax: (08) 8232 3994

Society of Women Writers   Women writers,
3 Brandt Street   playwrights, poets, TV,
Flagstaff Hill SA 5159   radio and print media
Ph: (08) 8370 7660   journalists
Fax: (08) 8370 7661

Victorian Fellowship of *Australian Writers* PO Box 528 Camberwell Vic 3124 Ph/Fax: (03) 9349 3722	Writers
Victorian Writers' Centre 156 George Street Fitzroy Vic 3065 Ph: (03) 9415 1077 Fax: (03) 9415 1080	Authors and writers
WA Writers' Centre 11 Old York Road Greenmount WA 6056 Ph: (09) 294 1872	Writers
Women in Publishing PO Box 1515 North Sydney NSW 2059 Ph: (02) 9954 1438 25 Loma Street Cottesloe WA 6001	Women at all levels in all areas of publishing

New Zealand

Special interest group	Members
Book Publishers Association *of NZ Inc (BPANZ)* PO Box 36–477 Northcote, Auckland 1309 Ph: (09) 480 2711 Fax: (09) 480 1130	Publishers – individuals, partnerships or companies engaged in the publishing of books, scholarly journals, educational material and multi-media works as a bona fide and continuing operation
Booksellers New Zealand Book House 86 Boulcott Street (PO Box 11–377) Wellington Ph: (04) 472 8678 Fax: (04) 472 8628	Booksellers – independent, franchise, would-be bookshop owners and suppliers of goods and services to booksellers

Children's Literature Association of NZ Inc PO Box 26–020 Epsom, Auckland Ph: (09) 524 2767	Writers, publishers and individuals interested in children's literature
Christian Booksellers Association of NZ PO Box 4017 New Plymouth 4615 Ph/Fax: (06) 758 4912	Booksellers of Christian literature
Friends of the Dorothy Neal White Collection PO Box 12–499 Wellington North	Researchers, writers
Friends of the Turnbull Library PO Box 12–186 Wellington North	Researchers, writers
Listener Women's Book Festival Booksellers New Zealand Book House PO Box 11–377 Wellington Ph: (04) 472 8678 Fax: (04) 472 8628	Women writers and publishers
Montana New Zealand Book Awards Booksellers New Zealand Book House PO Box 11–377 Wellington Ph: (04) 472 8678 Fax: (04) 472 8628	Booksellers, publishers and writers
New Zealand Book Council Ph: (04) 499 1569 Fax: (04) 499 1424	Publishers, booksellers, writers and editors

New Zealand Book Editors'
Association
PO Box 99–259
Newmarket, Auckland
Ph: (09) 360 0412

Writers, editors, publishers

New Zealand Children's
Book Foundation
PO Box 96–094
Balmoral, Auckland
Ph/Fax: (09) 620 5459

Booksellers, teachers,
librarians, students of
literature, publishing and
editing, and those
interested in children's
books

New Zealand Library and
Information Association: Te
Rau Herenga o Aotearoa
Level 8, 86 Lambton Quay
(PO Box 12–212)
Wellington
Ph: (04) 473 5834
Fax: (04) 499 1480

Librarians, booksellers,
publishers, editors, writers,
students of literature and
researchers

NZ Post Children's Book
Festival
John Barr
Booksellers New Zealand
Book House
PO Box 11–377
Wellington
Ph: (04) 472 8678
Fax: (04) 472 8628

Children's writers,
publishers and booksellers

New Zealand Reading
Association
Sheena Hervey
Dunedin College of Education
Private Bag
Dunedin

Readers and writers

New Zealand Society of
Authors (Pen NZ Inc)
PO Box 67–013
Mt Eden, Auckland 3
Ph/Fax: (09) 630 8077

Published and unpublished
writers

New Zealand Writers Guild   Writers
Lower Level, 300 Richmond
Road
Grey Lynn
(PO Box 46–018)
Herne Bay, Auckland
Ph/Fax: (09) 360 1527

13 Recommended reading

Books

Australian Booksellers Association, *Directory of Members 1996-97*, Australian Booksellers Association, Carlton, 1996. (An annual publication)

Australian Bureau of Statistics, *Books: Who's Reading Them Now? A Study of Book Buying and Borrowing in Australia*, Australia Council, Strawberry Hills, 1995.

Australian Government Publishing Service, *Style Manual for Authors, Editors and Printers*, 5th edition, AGPS Press, Canberra, 1994.

Australian Publishers Association, *Directory of Members 1997-98*, Australian Publishers Association, Ultimo, 1997. (An annual publication)

Australian Writers' Dictionary, OUP, Melbourne, 1997.

Baverstock, A., *Are Books Different? Marketing in the Book Trade*, Kogan Page, London, 1993.

——, *How to Market Books*, 2nd edition, Kogan Page, London, 1997.

Bolles, R.N., *What Color is Your Parachute? A Practical Manual for Job-Hunters and Career-Changers*, Ten Speed Press, Berkeley, California, updated yearly.

The Chicago Manual of Style, 14th edition, University of Chicago Press, Chicago, 1993.

Clark, G., *Inside Book Publishing*, 2nd edition, Blueprint, London, 1994.

Copyediting: The Cambridge Handbook for Editors, Authors and Publishers, 3rd edition, Cambridge University Press, 1992.

Davies, Gill, *Book Commissioning and Acquisition*, Routledge, 1994.

Derricourt, R., *Ideas into Books: A guide to scholarly non-fiction publishing*, Penguin, 1996.

Dutton, G., *A Rare Bird: Penguin Books in Australia 1946–96*, Penguin Books, Ringwood, 1997.

D.W. Thorpe, *Australian Literary Awards and Fellowships*, 2nd edition, D.W. Thorpe, Melbourne, 1993.

Eyler, D., *Resumés that Mean Business*, Random House, New York, 1990.

Ferguson, Dale Shaw. *Marketing Yourself to Employers: A step by step guide to getting the job you want*, Hale & Iremonger, Sydney, 1996.

Flann, E. and Hill, B., *The Australian Editing Handbook*, AGPS Press, Canberra, 1994.

Foley, Bernadette, *Beatrice Davis Editorial Fellowship 1997 Report*, Australian Publishers Association, 1997 (www.publishers.asn.au).

Forsyth, Patrick, *Marketing in Publishing*, Routledge, 1997.

Fowler, H.W., *A Dictionary of Modern English*, 2nd edition, rev. by Sir Ernest Gowers, Oxford University Press, Oxford, 1983.

Harts Rules for Compositors and Readers at the University Press, 39th edition, Oxford University Press, Oxford, 1983.

Healy, L., *My First Year in Publishing*, Walker & Company, New York, 1994.

Hudson, N., *Modern Australian Usage*, Oxford University Press, Melbourne, 1993.

Huggett, R., *The Wit of Publishing*, W.H. Allen, London, 1986.

Kaplan, C., *Publish for Profit: How to write, market and promote your own book*, Cyndi Kaplan Communications, 1997.

Kirsch, J., *Kirsch's Handbook of Publishing Law for Authors, Publishers, Editors and Agents*, Acrobat Books, Los Angeles, 1995.

Margaret Gee's Media Guide, Information Australia. (Updates published regularly)

Murray-Smith, S., *Right Words: A Guide to Modern English Usage*, 2nd edition, Penguin Books, Ringwood, 1990.

New Zealand Books in Print 1997, 25th edition, Heinemann, 1997.

Phillips, M. and Rasberry, S., *Marketing Without Advertising Creative Strategies for Small Business Success*, 7th edition, Nolo Press, Berkeley, California, 1992.

Plotnik, A., *The Elements of Editing: A Modern Guide for Editors and Journalists*, Macmillan, 1979.

Rosenberg, J., *Dictionary of Marketing and Advertising*, John Wiley & Sons, New York, 1995.

Schwarz, Samantha, *Australian Guide to Getting Published*, Hale & Iremonger, Sydney, 1995.

Strunk, W. Jr and White, E. B., *The Elements of Style*, 3rd edition, Macmillan, New York, 1979.

Unwin, S., *The Truth about Publishing*, George Allen & Unwin, London, 1928.

Veitch, K., *Real Live Writers — How to Host a Successful Author Visit*, National Book Council, Carlton, 1995.

White, K. and White, F., *Display and Visual Merchandising*, St Francis Press, Westwood, 1996.

——, *Independent Bookstore Planning and Design*, St Francis Press, Westwood, 1993.

Whouley, K., Miller, L., and Hawkins, R., *Manual on Bookselling: Practical Advice for the Bookstore Professional*, 5th Edition, American Booksellers Association, Tarrytown, 1996.

Journals

All book reviews in the *Age, Herald-Sun, Sydney Morning Herald, Courier Mail, West Australian, Australian, Listener, North and South, Metro, NZ Books* etc.

American Bookseller

Australian Book Review (National Book Council)

Australian Bookseller & Publisher (D.W. Thorpe)

Australian Editor, Blue Pencil (NSW), Society of Editors (Victoria) Newsletter, etc (Contact your state's Society of Editors)

Australian Review of Books (Published by the *Australian,* second Wednesday of the month)

Australian Women's Book Review

The Bookseller (UK weekly, available from D.W. Thorpe)

Booksellers News (New Zealand)

The Bulletin (in particular 'Patricia Rolfe's Book Bulletin')

NB (Magazine of the ABA)

The New Zealand Author (Society of Authors)

The Publisher (New Zealand)

Publishers' Weekly (USA weekly, available from D.W. Thorpe)

Publishing Studies (Department of Communications Studies, RMIT)

14 Glossary

Similar to other professions, the book trade has a language all of its own. Once you learn the terms and jargon, you will find that speaking and listening to people in the industry and reading the trade journals will become more interesting and informative.

ABA Australian Booksellers Association, a must to join once you become a bookseller. The ABA provides training seminars, runs the Certificate of Bookshop Practice as well as an annual conference, a monthly newsletter and acts in the interests of booksellers with publishers and government regarding issues that affect their members.

ABR *Australian Book Review*, an excellent monthly reviews journal, published by the National Book Council.

advance copy A copy of a forthcoming title sent to booksellers and book reviewers prior to the release date.

all rights reserved Any material within that publication cannot be reproduced in any way without consent from the copyright owner.

annual Book or magazine published once a year.

anthology A collection of writings in a similar genre.

APA The Australian Publishers Association, formed in 1948, has a membership of approximately 150 publishers.

Australian Bookseller & Publisher The monthly book trade magazine — essential reading.

back list The older titles on a publisher's list that are still in print.

back order Any titles not supplied by the distributor or publisher on the shop's original order may be kept on back order to be supplied when available.

Baker & Taylor Largest US-based book wholesaler.

Banjo Awards National Book Council Awards for the titles considered the best Australian books published that year.

BBIP British Books in Print.

Blad Book Layout And Design. Often used as a sales tool by sales reps to show booksellers what the finished title will look like.

Blue Newsletter Also known by its correct title of the *Weekly Book Newsletter*. This weekly newsletter carries news of publisher moves/amalgamations, book promotions, seminars and employment opportunities and is also essential reading.

blurb A publisher's description of the book that appears on the back of the cover or jacket or on the inside flap of a dust jacket.

Booker Prize Considered the most important British award for fiction, the Booker is awarded in October and is often controversial.

bound Hardcover book.

Bowker USA publisher offering trade journals and books in print listing.

buy in An order placed with a publisher's sales representative for new releases.

CBC Children's Book Council of Australia. Oversees the annual prestigious CBC awards announced in July.

CD-ROM Compact Disk Read Only Memory listing books in print and is an alternative to microfiche.

closed market When a publisher has exclusive rights to a particular book or imprint.

consignment Titles which remain the property of the publisher and is paid for by the bookseller upon its being sold.

discount The percentage discount subtracted from the rrp (recommended retail price) by the publisher or distributor when selling to the bookseller.

distributor A person who acts as a wholesaler for publishers and sells titles to booksellers.

Ditmars Awards voted on and presented by members of the Australian National Science Fiction Convention. Also known as the Australian Science Fiction Achievement Awards.

dummy Mock-up of a book.

dumpbin Publisher's point of sale floor display bin in a bookshop containing multiple copies of a title.

dust jacket Paper cover to protect and attract attention to a hardbound book.

D.W. Thorpe Publisher of *AB&P* and the *Weekly Book Newsletter.*

editor In the broadest sense, this is the person who edits the manuscript and prepares the text for publicity. In a more specialised sense, the *commissioning editor* is the 'talent scout' who commissions manuscripts for their publishing house; the *structural editor* is concerned with the overall structure of the text rather than the specifics of grammar, etc.; and the *copy editor* corrects manuscripts, checks punctuation, spelling, syntax and grammar.

endpapers Blank pages at the front and back of a book adjacent to the cover.

errata When an error is found in the text of a title after the title has been published, the corrections if thought justified by the publisher are printed on a loose sheet of paper and inserted in to the book.

face out Displaying the title on the shelf with the cover (rather than the spine) facing outwards.

firm sale Sold to the bookseller as a non-returnable title — often at a higher discount than a sale or return title.

format The physical form of a book, its trim-size and shape (ie: paperback or hard cover, CD-ROM or audio tape).

front list New titles released by a publisher.

frontispiece Illustration facing the title of book, i.e. on page 2.

galley proof Printer's proof before the final edit of the title.

impression A reprint made without changes to the text.

imprint The publisher's ID or a particular series of books. i.e. an imprint of Penguin is the children's series Puffin.

indent Titles from an overseas publisher or distributor.

ISBN International Standard Book Number. A method used by publishers, booksellers, libraries and other book agencies to identify titles.

ISSN International Standard Serial Number used for serial publications, such as magazines and journals.

local agent Australian agent for an overseas publisher or distributor.

loss leader A title that is sold at a huge discount (sometimes to the booksellers' loss) in order to attract customers into the bookshop.

misbound A book that has been misbound such that pages are missing, appear in the wrong order or are upside down, or are poorly bound so that pages fall out.

Montana Awards for excellence in New Zealand publishing and design.

NBC National Book Council.

new release New title releases from the publisher.

no fault return A title returned due to no fault of the booksellers such as it being misbound.

NOP Not our publication.

NYP Not Yet Published.

OP Out of Print.

OS Out of stock at the publisher.

paperback Soft-cover book.

proforma Payment in advance.

proof copy Often unedited copy of a title made available to booksellers and reviewers before publication.

pull Section (chapter) of a new book made available for booksellers to sample. *See* blad.

point of sale material Also known as POS. Publishers promotional items such as poster, shelf talkers, dumpbins, mobiles, cut-outs, etc. to assist the bookseller to promote their titles.

remainders Books which are unsold by the publisher or distributor that are then *remaindered* to booksellers, that is, sold at a price well under standard discount in order to clear them from the publisher's shelves.

RP Reprinting — New printing of a book once it has been sold out.

RPUC Reprint under consideration by publisher.

returns Books that are sold on a sale or return basis and can be returned to the publisher after 3 months but before 6 months.

sales representative A person who visits booksellers on a regular basis to show new releases, re-order back list, authorise returns and conduct general business on behalf of a publisher or distributor.

shelf talker A strip of card that sits on a shelf to attract customers towards the titles that sit above it.

small order surcharge Extra charge for delivery when an order does not meet the minimum order criteria.

title Name given to a manuscript or book.

Vogel 'The Vogel' or The *Australian*/Vogel National Literary Award is an annual prize of $15,000 promoted by the *Australian*, sponsored by Vogel's bread and awarded to a writer under 35 years for an original unpublished manuscript of fiction or Australian history or biography. The winner is guaranteed publication by Allen & Unwin.

Weekly Book Newsletter Also known as the 'Blue Newsletter' in Australia, this is a weekly newsletter that carries news of publisher moves/amalgamations, book promotions, seminars and employment opportunities and is essential reading for those in the book trade.

Women's Book Festival The *Listener*'s New Zealand festival celebrating women's writing, publishing and reading.

15 Interview with Bob Sessions

Publisher, Penguin Books Australia

How did you get into publishing?
Unorthodoxly. After I left school I wanted to be the commodore of the P&O Shipping Company. So I went to the University of Southhampton and did a course.

What sort of course?
A course in navigation, marine engineering, astronomy, that sort of thing. I did all right in the course and I actually joined P&O and had three or four years at sea. During that time I realised that life at sea was a very strange thing to do for the rest of my life and that most 40-year-olds at sea were either paranoids or drunks. And I thought that really I wanted to get out while I was young enough to do something else. I had read a number of books on publishing and writing and one of these was a book called *A Profession for Gentlemen* by Frederick Warburg. It was a pretty romantic view of the trade because he came from a very rich family and spent a lot of time having lunch and reading wonderful books and meeting exciting authors, and I thought, 'This is the life for me. It sounds too good to be true'. I wanted to be a publisher, but I didn't really know what it meant. So I went to see a friend of my father's who was a publisher in London and he began to clue me into the realities. He said, 'If you really want to be a publisher we get applications from Oxford and Cambridge undergraduates, from teachers and booksellers, which one are you?' and I said, 'None of the above'. And he said, 'Well, I can't really help you

then'. And I left his office and thought I *could* be a bookseller, I couldn't really get into Oxford or Cambridge, and I couldn't be a teacher. So I went around to a few bookshops and in those days it wasn't so difficult to get a job in a bookshop, although it was badly paid, I think about £5 a week. I managed to get a position at the Times Bookshop in Wigmore Street. It was a very up-market bookshop. I started in the basement, sorting stock, then moved up to atlases, then globes, then poetry and then after about a year I went to the front of the shop, where I met very interesting people, including Paul Hamlyn and other luminaries of the book trade. And I thought, 'I could really go back and see that guy now'. So I went back to Hutchinson and said, 'I've done some bookselling and I still want to be in publishing'. And he said, 'Well, you are in luck my boy, we have just started an apprenticeship scheme. I can't pay you very much money, but if you would like to start on Monday I'll give you an apprenticeship for a year'. And so I started in publishing and I earned £7 a week.

So £2 more than you were getting?
Yes. So I thought that was wonderful, and I was very lucky.

What did the apprenticeship involve, was it a formal course of study?
No, it was on-the-job training. It started in Sir Robert Lusty's outside office (he was the chairman). Running errands, taking messages and then I started to move from department to department. About three or four months with Marketing, three or four months with Sales, Foreign Rights, Editorial and so on. In about thirteen or fourteen months I came back to his office and he said, 'Well, I have had a report on you from each of the departments and I have decided that the best place for you is in Editorial. You can start in the foreign-language side of Editorial, where we buy and sell translation rights.' So I went to work in this job. I really enjoyed it, it was exciting, I even got a small pay increase. And then one day, a friend of mine said, 'I am going to drive to Australia'. And I said that wasn't possible, because it was surrounded by water; I'd been there. And he said, 'Well I'm going to drive as far as possible, do you want to come?' And I said, 'No, I don't think so, I'm happy here. I've seen the world'. He said, 'I know that you've seen the outside of many countries, but don't you want to see the inside?' (very clever as it turned out). So anyway I bought

a share in the Landrover, did the big trip, and ended up in Australia almost by accident after many adventures. Later, I found my way to Melbourne, where all the publishing was in those days. All the English publishing houses had their branch offices in Melbourne. I went to see Nelson, Cassell, Oxford, Macmillan, Hutchinson and to my amazement, they all offered me a job because I had had this front-line training. And, not only just any old job, but at Cassell they offered me 'the' job as editor of their Australian operation, and in one of those brave moments I said, 'Yes, I could do that'. So I was given a desk and a telephone and they said, 'Off you go, do some publishing'. Fortunately, they didn't know any more about it than I did. So we all learnt together on the job!

How did the reality of publishing stand up to the fantasy?
Maybe because I was in a foreign country at that stage, maybe because I had been given this huge opportunity, maybe because other people were terribly kind to me, it was in fact a very exciting time. I got to meet authors who were just names to me, Tom Keneally, Peter Mathers, Patrick White. I made friends with a journalist in Melbourne. Her name was Nan Hutton, she worked on *The Age* and she knew her way around, and she was like a literary godmother to me in many ways. I also made friends with a man named Arthur Stokes from Wilke, the printers. And I guess when I didn't know something I just found someone who did, and went and picked their brains! It was actually very exciting, but also very hard work and I made lots of very terrible mistakes. But fortunately, the people I worked with didn't know any more than I did, so generally I got away with it.

And how long have you worked with Penguin, because you have worked with Penguin a couple of times, haven't you?
Yes, after about seven or eight years at Cassell I was approached by Penguin's John Hooker who said, 'Hilary McPhee is leaving us and we have a job, do you want it?' And I said, 'Oh, I don't think I want to drive all the way out to Ringwood, and be an editor working for you, when I'm the publisher here at Cassell'. But anyway, he was very persuasive, he painted Penguin very well as the best place to be, and convinced me I could have an exciting future there. Once again I made one of those leaps of faith and thought, 'Well what do I have to lose really?' I joined Penguin and I was working with

John on the Australian list and I was there for about seven years before I went off to Nelson with John Michie. And when I came back to Penguin again, by quite a different route in 1987, Brian Johns was the publisher, closely followed by Susan Ryan and when Susan left I was offered the job of publisher. It was really the job I always wanted, and this time I've been there for about ten years.

What are the different tasks involved in your job?
Let me go back a step. In order to understand my answer you have to understand how I see my job. I see my job as being responsible for ensuring that Penguin Australia has a viable, exciting publishing program for next year. It is always *next* year. So much of my life is geared to the future. Someone like me is only as good as their next year's program. On the one hand, my day is spent helping people solve problems that are happening now, jackets that have gone wrong, authors who are having difficulties for one reason or another, something being lost, a printing job that's gone wrong. But much of my intellectual energy is spent on planning what we are going to be doing in the year ahead, or even years ahead. So my day is a combination, I am reacting to the present, but also planning for and working in the future. Working for a big company like Penguin, I have been able to departmentalise and I have wonderful people working with me and for me; a publisher for the adult books; a publisher for the children's books; a publisher for our travel section; and people running production, rights and design. They take care of the day-to-day requirements of those positions. But as publishing director the ultimate responsibility for the publishing program rests with me. My relationship with them is incredibly important; they generally know when they need to refer to me and when they don't. A lot of time is spent in discussion with those people, helping make the right decision, testing assumptions, making sure that they have made the necessary connection to the other parts of the company, in order for each project to be a success. Also in meetings. Some people have this wonderfully cavalier attitude towards meetings: 'Oh, I don't like meetings, I hate going to them, they are a waste of time'. Meetings per se are not a waste of time; the right meetings, that is. We have a particular meeting at Penguin, every Tuesday, called the Program Meeting and it goes for several hours and around the table sit thirteen or fourteen people with enormous experience

of publishing. It's one of the engines of our success, because it is where all the day-to-day skills come together: marketing, administration, sales, editorial, finance. You might say, 'Oh, don't they just end up with conflicting decisions?' and the answer is no, because each department brings its own particular skills and applies those to the project, idea or program. In all good publishing companies, publishing decisions are made by publishers and not by a committee; so the editors make decisions about *what* we publish, but then the committee comes into its own when we decide *how* we'll publish it; what the right format should be; what the right price should be; how many we should produce; what sort of marketing we should apply; and that's where I think a great advantage comes from all that experience and talent.

My day is also spent dealing with and assisting authors, because we have many, and you have to look after those whose books we publish because there'll be other books from them one day; also dealing with agents, who are bringing us many of our new books and ideas, corresponding with our own company overseas via mail and e-mail, and generally doing that stewardship role which helps each department to do its job to the best of its ability; asking questions, encouraging, going round the building and just being a part of it all and spreading enthusiasm! Somebody has to get the priorities in view, and in a fairly big department like mine — there are some sixty-five people in the publishing department, from production, editorial, design and so on — with a staff of that size, one relies on one's management enormously, but also you've got to step back two paces and say, 'Have we got our priorities right today; what are the *most important things* to be done?' I think it's very much part of my job to say, 'Today I must achieve say three things', whatever they are, and they must be things which are of most importance to our future. So I guess I spend a bit of my time on that sort of intellectual exercise of saying, 'What's important?' rather than just 'What's in my in-tray today?'

And do you have a lot of hands-on work with particular titles, or do you mostly delegate it?
What is delegated is the business of actually turning the material into a book. One of the most critical parts of being a publisher however (and it pre-empts your question about the best advice given to me, so I'll answer that one now) was

instilled in me by one of my great publishing gurus, a man named Lloyd O'Neil, with whom I worked very closely for a few years; a marvellous man who had been a bookseller and publisher and was a great enthusiast and contributor to the book trade. He taught me a very important lesson early on. He said that when we're talking about a concept, an idea, a pile of manuscript, whatever it is, you must take yourself forward and become the rep, who's going to sell that book to the bookseller in its final form. In other words, he wanted me to visualise the cover, the binding, the number of pages, the retail price. If you can learn to do that, have a vision that will inform all of your decisions on the way through, then that's a wonderful ability because that's ideally the way to approach every project. I *boringly* say to people, 'What's the *title*?' and they say, 'It doesn't matter yet', and I say, 'It *does* matter, and it's going to matter even more very soon', and I say, 'What's the format?' and they say, 'We'll work on that' and I say, 'No, let's think about it now, because the decision we make about that will inform every other decision'. So, I think a lot of the time, I'm taking the project through in my head, visualising all the things that can happen on the way through, and then make sure that they do. You can delegate most things, but you can't always delegate the vision. The vision comes from the publisher.

And what's the best thing about your job (apart from being taken out for lunch)?
Oh, I don't know, it's corny I suppose . . . But it's true for me as I'm sure it is for everybody in the industry; that I love the business of books; I love being around books, buying books, reading books, putting them in bookshelves and enjoying their success. I also enjoy the thrill of the chase, the uncertainty, the gambling element, that it can go terribly right or terribly wrong, and also the people. One of the great things about being in the publishing industry is that you tend to work with people who are like yourself who have the same kinds of interests. It's very much, as you know, a people industry. I often imagine being in other industries, which I know very little about, and I wonder whether the people are as interesting and fun to be with, and I suspect that they're not! The best part is the books and the second best part is the people.

Someone once said to me that you get into the publishing

industry because you like books but you stay in it because you like the people.
I'm sure that's true. There's also another thing, and that is that publishing is a rather arcane world; it's hard to describe it to people who don't know it. Most people think that we're printers, or booksellers or something. And what we actually do is quite hard to come to grips with. It takes a while to learn, and when you have learnt it, like anything else I suppose, there is a great confidence and enjoyment in doing what you do well, and understanding what it is you do and how it all works. And one of the great pleasures in my kind of role is that you're able to dabble in marketing, sales, bookselling, design and editorial, so it's a very eclectic life, which suits me. Every book is different. If you're making bread or nuts and bolts, tomorrow's very much like today, I imagine. But not in our lives, where every day something exciting happens, and it gives you the necessary adrenalin.

As you know, there are many publishing courses available at the moment. Do you want to make any comment about all these people rushing off to do publishing courses, and on what value they are to the industry?
Well, the first thing I'd say is that I think they are absolutely essential. I'm a great believer in formal, professional education. If anything I think that for too long anyone could become a publisher (like me!) and all that was required was a love of books. It's a highly professional business these days, and it should be even more professional than it is, and one of the things these courses help bring to the industry is that professionalism. I've been a supporter of the RMIT course and I've been on the advisory committee for quite some time and I think it's a very good course. I'm sure the others are also extremely good in their way. I think that the people need to go to those courses with a reasonably sound educational background and a level of enthusiasm and *some* contact with the trade. As you know, the RMIT course has the requirement that they already be in the trade. If they do all those things, they will benefit enormously from a two-year part-time course. I think I can honestly say that most of the people we've employed in our publishing department in the last three or four years have been through one of those courses. But we haven't employed them *because* they've been through the course, we've employed them because they are *better* candi-

dates than the others, and I believe the courses have helped them to be better.

Lots of people must say to you, 'I'd love to work in publishing, I'd love to be an editor, love to be a publisher'. What advice do you have for those people?
My advice is always: Before you make a final decision, get a bit closer to it. It's rather like the advice I was given myself when I was twenty years old, which was go and do something which is involved with books in some way to make sure you're really making the right decision. Bookselling is a great starting point. I've always thought that. But there are many others; you can work in magazines, you can work in book distribution or marketing. Being involved in some way in the book trade means you know enough about it to say 'I know it's badly paid, I know it demands an awful lot of me, but it is really what I want to do'. Once you've made that decision, then you can think about what sort of qualifications you need and which branch of the business will suit you best. The first thing you need is to be adept with words, and you must be good at communicating because if you're not, you should be doing something else. If you are a natural communicator and you can support that with a sound educational background, then the next thing you need, in addition to a little bit of experience, is a qualification. During the course, the realities of your abilities will become clear, if not to you, at least to your tutors!

Are there any other comments you'd like to make about careers or publishing?
I think one of the very important things to understand is that it is a multi-faceted industry, and it requires expertise in all sorts of areas. Our industry will only become more professional and more successful if we have that level of expertise across the departments. We need administrators; we need expert, talented booksellers; we need people in marketing and sales who understand books and bookselling. We need people who are good at editing and who understand that that's what they're good at, and don't necessarily want to be anything else. We need people who understand what it means to be a publisher and not an editor, because the talents are different. And I think that once we understand that bookselling is a true profession, as the Germans do for example, and not just something nice to spend your time doing, we can then segment

it and say, 'I am going to be the very best there is at book marketing', or at book production, or in editorial or design, or at finance, and each contributes to the whole.

As you know, Alison, most people, when they think of publishing, say things like, 'Oh, it must be awfully nice to sit there reading books all day', or 'How do you find time to read all of those manuscripts?', or 'I've always liked design, I'm sure I could design a good book cover' and nothing is or should be that simple. It's just like saying 'I've always thought I could write a book'; writing books isn't easy, writing books is terribly difficult, as is writing music or painting a canvas. And being a publisher isn't easy. It's very difficult these days when the market's flat and the competition is at its greatest and when there's more retail space than ever before, but no more buyers, and our skills are being really tested. Those people with dedication and training, who are prepared to put in the long hours are succeeding in this very difficult market, and that's the way it should be. And if people want to succeed, they've got to become very good at what they've set out to do. Being very good requires a lot of dedication; it also requires training, it requires putting in the long hours and continually testing oneself against the best.

16 Interview with Anna Bolger

Promotions Manager, Lonely Planet Publications

Anna, you're now the promotions manager at Lonely Planet. How did you get here, did you always want to work in publishing or was it serendipity, and what steps did you take to get where you are now?

I was studying Arts/Commerce at university and for the first few years I didn't know what I wanted to do. Maybe it was spending so much time around libraries and books, but it gradually came to me that publishing was what I wanted to do. I finished my degree and knew that it was difficult to get into publishing, so I rang up some people I knew in the industry, as well as some I didn't know, and asked them questions about how to get into publishing and what skills they would look for. The advice I was given, and this will date me, was that I should subscribe to the Blue Newsletter and learn to type, as opposed to now when people are probably saying you should know Netscape and Microsoft Access. I took this advice and I then applied for any job in the Blue Newsletter. At that stage I really just wanted to work in publishing and I suppose I hadn't given that much thought to what I actually wanted to do. Having done an Arts degree, I could probably have gone into editing, or indeed publicity, where I've ended up. The first job that I got was a part-time position as a publicity assistant.

At which publishing house was that?
That was with J.M. Dent, who then became Houghton-Mifflin and later Jacaranda Wiley.

And how did you end up at Lonely Planet, were you still working with Dent when they went into Jacaranda Wiley, or were you working somewhere else in between?
I went overseas after Houghton-Mifflin closed. When I returned there was a job advertised with Longmans, and there was also a job advertised at Lonely Planet, so I applied for them both. Longmans got back to me and I was lucky enough to get that job, meanwhile Lonely Planet were still processing the application. Then lo-and-behold Lonely Planet rang and asked me to come in for an interview, which happened to be on my first day at Longmans. The job at Lonely Planet sounded more interesting and was a step up from where I'd been, as opposed to the Longmans job which was in publicity and administration. I got the Lonely Planet position, helped by the fact that I had just been overseas, plus my employment background. I've been at Lonely Planet now for five years.

And what's a typical day at Lonely Planet?
A typical day is my phone constantly ringing, either internal or external calls! There's only myself in our promotions department, so I have to do everything. When I say that I'm not being a martyr, but you've got to be prepared to pack books and stuff envelopes, attend functions and arrange launches, go to book fairs, organise the stand and deal with the media. We get a lot of calls from people who need information, so much of my job involves work that you can't anticipate, created by projects that come in and have to be done either that day or that week. The media might want information on the company for a story they're doing, or students doing an MBA assignment might ring. Plus, we are constantly releasing new editions or new titles, so there are media releases and review copies to go out. The directors, Tony and Maureen Wheeler, are notable people in Australian publishing and business circles and we get a lot of calls and emails from people wanting to talk to them or our other authors. Lonely Planet has offices in London, California and Paris, but Melbourne is the head office, so a lot of the overseas promotional material and information is organised by me.

And do you get lots of people saying to you, 'Oh, you're so

lucky to work in publishing', seeming to think you have a charmed job?
They do think that with publishing and Lonely Planet too. A lot of people think I must travel a lot because Lonely Planet publish travel guides. I do a lot of interstate travel with Lonely Planet and I've been fortunate enough to have a couple of overseas trips, but the people who actually do the travel are quite separate from the people in the office. However, I am very fortunate that Lonely Planet is a company that suits my style.

Well, it is a funky, hip company!
Yes, although now that it's getting bigger it has to be more structured and corporate, even though that's a word that Lonely Planet hates to use.

It is a business, though . . .
It *is* a business, it's there to make money. The competition is tough, so we can't be lackadaisical about what we do.

And do you get a lot of people sending in CVs and applications out of the blue?
Yes, we certainly do. People who have no relevant tertiary studies or practical experience, but they've travelled and they've used Lonely Planet guides and they'd like to be a part of the Lonely Planet company.

What sort of thing do you like to see in CVs?
It depends on the level at which they're coming in, but the primary criterion for us would be travel: travel experience using Lonely Planet. So independent sort of people interested in other cultures and the environment are key criteria. I say depending on the level, because it may be a person's first job and they may not have had the opportunity to travel, so we don't want to discount them, but nonetheless we'd be looking for some kind of interest in travel or other cultures in their CV. Computer literacy is important: we're a very computer-oriented company. I think we were one of the first publishing companies to have a computer on every staff member's desk, and we've been doing that for many years now. So they've got to have good computer skills, that's for sure. Much of the editorial and cartographic work is done in teams, so they've got to be a team player and believe in the product. They also

need the relevant editing and cartographic skills, or publicity or marketing experience.

Being able to back up experience and skills with achievements?
Yes, unless we're looking for a trainee.

And what are the common aspects that people seem to focus on in CVs that don't have any relevance at all?
Well, I've read résumés where people don't mention the company at all. I know the job situation's bad, so you're probably sending off a hundred form letters for a marketing assistant or customer service position, but I think you need to mention the company's name somewhere in your letter . . .

To prove that it's not the same letter you sent to another publisher?
Yes, I've read job applications for a job with us, and they've said, 'I'd like to work for company X' and written the name of another company! That's sloppy. I think they've got to mention the name of the company to show that they know something about what the company does. You can read a résumé and tell when an applicant has no idea what you do.

And with your World Wide Web page, for which you are constantly winning accolades, it's not as though they can't get through to the information.
I think they've got to do a bit of research about the company because we do ask what they know about us. People might say, 'Well, I used your USA guide', and we're thinking, 'Well, we don't really have a USA guide'. And that has happened! We are not talking about heaps of study, but if you want a job with a company you've got to show some interest in what they do, even if it's not your dying interest, but just to show that you've got initiative. So that then we can think, 'Well, they do care a bit because they've actually made an effort to know something about us'. And I've also read applications where the letter will tell me, 'I've done this-that-and-the-other in this job blah-blah-blah' and then you turn over to the actual résumé and the information in it doesn't back up what the letter has said. Obviously, to present yourself you need to put in a 110 per cent effort, but I've read letters where they say, 'I've written press releases and I've liaised with the media and I've got Word and Excel and Powerpoint and I did this at Company A, and at Company B I did customer service.' Then

you turn over to the résumé and they've written 'Company A, 1992 to 1993', but there's no reference to what was in the covering letter. The inconsistency makes me think they are being more honest in the résumé, whereas they're writing the letter in relation to the ad. Quite often, I would suspect, this is because the résumé is standardised, but they target the letter to the job. It makes you think, 'Well, all I've got at the moment is this résumé to rely on, so therefore what is this person telling me? What message are they giving me?'

So do you always check up on references?
Yes, we do.

And if the people have a qualification, do you check up with the institution? Do you give computer or typing tests?
Certainly if it's editorial, they'll get a typing test and an editorial test, and in cartography and design they give tests as well.

What's the best career advice anyone ever gave you?
You've got to think about the fact that wherever the company's logo appears it's their reputation but it's also your own, particularly as a publicist. You have to have all the publicity skills, but, at the end of the day, you've got to be honest and come across as an honest and reliable person.

Someone with integrity?
Yes, I really think so. If the media sees you to be stretching the truth all the time, they won't have anything to do with you, and why should they? They rely on you, and if you're not reliable, then it's their reputation on the line.

And there are always lots of competitors out there.
That's exactly right. I guess, my advice would be this, if you really want to do something, then you have to take a risk. To get into publishing in the first place I was going from full-time work to part-time and I knew that I'd probably have to get another job to pay the rent and live. I thought, 'I really want to do this, it's worth the risk of only having half the money that I had before and who knows what will happen?'

So you're saying, take the risks.
Yes, if you really want something. That's where you really work 150 per cent and if you do that, I reckon the rewards are there. That paid off with me: this job was only part-time

and it ended up being full-time because I just put in so much. By the same token, we had a work experience school student here and she put her head down, and worked really hard and smart and I said to her, 'If you want a part-time job after school, you've got it'. She earned it: it was all due to her hard work. Someone who is willing to put in the hours if necessary, be reliable, and is able to catch on to things, they're the valuable employees.

So it isn't so much a tertiary qualification that you're looking for, more a can-do attitude perhaps?
Well, certainly I look for both, although to be perfectly honest I would discard a tertiary qualification. I think that it's important because there are lots of other skills that you gain from study, but if you've got two people with equal education and skill levels, the one who makes the effort is the one who will get on.

Are there any other comments that you'd like to make about people wanting a career in publishing?
It's a tight industry to get into. I guess my only advice would be talk to people in the industry and see if you can get some part-time work experience. If you're at uni, work on the magazine, be the editor, deal with the printers, get as much background information as you can. Perhaps get a job in a bookshop, so you know books, you know reps, you know what an ISBN is, what a back order is, what a dissatisfied customer is! Get to know publishing information and the publishing sales pattern. I'm not saying this is an easy thing to do, but if you want to work in publishing, it's important to put something on your CV that says you've had something to do with books, other than bought them and read them. I mean we get lots of people who say, 'Oh, I love books, I want to work in publishing'. Well, I'm not employing someone to sit and read. It's like saying, 'I love travel, I love photography', it's a vacuous statement.

There's nothing significant in someone coming to you and saying, 'I love selling and dealing with the media and I love writing media releases'? Obviously, loving books is secondary to that.
Well, in our case it is, but I think there are very defined aspects to our business. Most people who work in publishing, no matter what their job, love the feel of a new book. They love

being involved in the production process and that's almost an innate thing in their nature. When people say, 'I love reading and I'd love to work in publishing', to me it says that they don't know much about publishing, and I would say go away and do some homework.

17 Interview with Susan Blackwell

Executive Director, Australian Publishers Association

How did you become the director of the Australian Publishers Association? Was it intentionally or was it a happy accident?
Very much intentional. Right from school I knew that I wanted to work with books. Initially I thought that it might be in a journalism direction, but then I went to Sydney University and did an Arts degree and completed those immensely practical subjects such as English literature, Modern History and French, which of course was a wonderful general education — but with no real application outside the ivory tower of the university. All through university I worked in bookshops, in fact I worked in a bookshop at school, during the school holidays; that's always been my love ... so that when I came out of uni, the options were teaching or a public service career or department of foreign affairs or publishing. Publishing sounded interesting — I thought I knew a bit about it, having worked in book-shops. I applied for a job at Harper & Row for Brian Wilder, and I got the job because I had worked in bookshops. I found out months later that there were 120 applicants for that job. It was woefully paid: I have no hesitation in telling you I was paid $12,000 a year — thousands below what all of my contemporaries were earning, but I had a sort of a cachet that (a) I was doing what I wanted to do and (b) it was an acceptable cocktail party conversation! But I did get the job because I had exactly the same qualifications as all the other applicants, possibly less, but I had worked in bookshops. So I worked at Harper & Row for a little over a year. It was a

very small firm with a small number of people and we all
pitched in and did all sorts of things and Brian Wilder was a
terrific mentor in that he introduced me (I was his personal
assistant) to sales and marketing, editorial, design, and the
printing and technology, such as they were. So, even though I
was there only for a year, it was a marvellous introduction
through a small firm into budgeting etc.: all the things that
drive a publishing company. It was also a multi-national; whilst
we thought we were an Australian island, every Friday we had
to send off reports to the head office in New York and to the
major agencies to be evenly distributed. It was a great firm,
in hindsight, to work for because we had a publishing program
— Brian was the publishing and the marketing director — and
we also had a distribution line, so we knew exactly what was
selling, what was not; the warehouse was a 'hop, skip and a
jump' outside, and the editorial and sales and marketing
opposite, so everything was very close. There was an educational arm, not primary and secondary, but tertiary and
reference, and trade as well. So, it was a marvellous introduction to all facets of the Australian publishing industry. And
Brian was also a marvellous person for taking me out and
introducing me to people in the industry; he was also active
in the United States Book Association. The USBA had as its
prime focus the collection of statistics from other US multina-
tional firms operating in Australia and in the successful
running of a Christmas party! My job was to collect statistics
and organise Christmas parties! But I did get involved and
quite interested in the politics of working for a very small but
tightly focused trade association. All of the members of the
USBA, I think, were members of the ABPA as it then was.
When the job came up at the ABPA, I looked at it with interest
and Brian encouraged me to apply; he could see I had some-
what outgrown Harper & Row, and *he* certainly wasn't going
to hold me back.

And what position did you move into at the ABPA?
It was a while ago now, I was assisting the director with the
export committee. Jenny Curtis worked on education and I
worked with Sandra Forbes, the then director on a range of
things, such as book bounty and export. As Sandra didn't have
a personal assistant, this was more of an administrative position. This involved working with the members of the ABPA
on the export committee, the bounty and printing committee,

lobbies that we had. We ran the very successful anti-sales tax campaigns in conjunction with the National Book Council back in the 1980s. So, working with a range of people within the industry, including printers on book bounty, booksellers on the anti-sales tax campaign, authors on public lending right matters. It was a very good introduction, and Sandra became a bit of a mentor for me too. It's terribly important for people to find a mentor and to latch on to that person almost limpet-like — well, not too claustrophobically, but to find somebody who will direct them, give their career a nudge in the right direction. So I've been fortunate to have Brian and Sandra.

And after that administrative role at the ABPA?
Sandra left, and I became assistant director. Then, Sandra's successor Jan Noble left and I became director.

So how long have you been director?
I've been director for eight years, which is quite a long time when you think about the enormous change in the Association. We've gone from being a three-and-a-half person office to a seven-person office. The range of activities that we encompass has developed and grown. When I joined we did no marketing. Now the Trade Publishing Committee, which has always been in the Association, is very marketing focused. The level of our statistical collection has become far more sophisticated. We collect monthly statistics across the sectors of the industry, so that people in the industry, no matter what sector they're working in, can benchmark their own sales against those of that entire sector. We do a lot of work with government. Once upon a time the aim of the industry was to keep government away. The industry has always revelled in the fact that there has been a minimum of government assistance. Government has become, particularly with the Cultural Nation initiative of the Keating Government, more closely involved with the Arts; the book publishing industry has always been a little bit idiosyncratic: is book publishing part of the Arts or is it an industry? When you're dealing with the Australia Council and the Literature Board you're very much one of the cultural groups in Australia, and a very successful, longstanding one. But, when you're dealing with government on book bounty matters, you're definitely an industry. You can be doing that simultaneously.

And of course you're running lots of training seminars as well?
That too has increased over the years. The industry has perceived that there is a lack there. The industry is a very generous
one in giving back to itself. When I talk to colleagues about
the industry, they are amazed at the generosity of people in
the publishing industry. If they put on training sessions, they
have to pay their speakers from within their own industry. We
make a point of definitely not doing that — it's a dangerous
precedent. In addition to which it would drive up the costs of
the seminars. The idea is to keep them cost effective, so that
not only can small firms pay to send people, but also individuals working within the industry can come along. An
important point to make is that our seminars are pitched only
at those working within the industry. It is still a highly desirable industry, even though the pay is not very good.

It's seen as very glamorous for some reason.
For some reason, yes. We still haven't got to the bottom of
this one! For the APA to run courses open to the public would
be highly lucrative for us, but we think it irresponsible.

It's really not what you're there to do is it?
It's not what we're here to do. We're here to increase the
qualifications, to act as a networking group, to increase the
knowledge of those working within the industry. We hold
seminars on printing and new technologies, for instance; highly
focused things like the latest editorial techniques. We're currently working with the Australia Council, putting together a
very structured program for senior editors. We're also terribly
conscious of not treading on the toes of the Society of Editors
training program too, because we recognise that it's an important fundraising activity for them. Also, the Galley Club — we
tend not to cross over there, although we will get together and
hold joint seminars with them. We like to work co-operatively
with other organisations in the industry: we cross-promote
things and hold joint things. That is a very important role for
the industry association to play.

**Do you get people contacting the APA looking for advice on
how to get into publishing?**
Yes, we do. We have to direct them, because a few have quite
unrealistic expectations, and I think that's where some of the
courses around are going to be quite helpful for them. Even

if they just look at the subjects offered in those courses. Even if they don't take the initiative and do those courses.

Even if they ring up the Media and Arts Alliance and find out what the pay rates are for editors, that's often enough to put people off.
They do that, do they?

Oh yes, I get people to do that if they ring me. I get a lot of lawyers for some reason.
Lawyers are paid incredible rates. But you're right about lawyers. The number of lawyers who actually do make the cross is quite interesting. There are quite a number of lawyers working in the publishing industry in a lot of areas. We have two lawyers in this office, who definitely do not practise as lawyers. Janice Field works on educational publishing. She works with the tertiary and professional committee and the educational committee which deals with primary and secondary publishing, and the small publishers committee. Her background is tax law, and you can understand why she left! I'm a lawyer, my background is intellectual property, and that is incredibly valuable for the job I do. In fact, it's almost a necessary qualification for being executive director of the Association.

Did you do your law course after you started here?
Yes. I did it part-time while I was director.

How long did it take to do that?
Four-and-a-half years. I was particularly interested in trade practices and copyright law, trademarks, and business reputation, those sorts of areas. Some of it can be useful — industrial relations — I'm very interested in that too. When I look around at the people who are doing my sort of job — people who run the collective societies and the trade associations in the artistic and entertainment area — just about every single one of them is a non-practising lawyer, which is really quite a reflection on how the arts and entertainment area has developed over the years. The need for lawyers, the impact of litigation and defamation for instance — particularly in publishing and contract law, the need to know your way around a contract — particularly when the copyright law does not, cannot, and never will, keep up with technological change. Therefore the importance of contract law becomes vital. So,

there are a number of lawyers who are actually running trade
associations, which is one of the reasons why I did a law
degree. I really did feel as though I was behind the eight ball,
and I'm feeling a lot better now. The trade association does
have to consult lawyers; we consult them on a range of matters,
unfortunately.

**If someone came to you and said, 'Susan, you've got the dream
job, how do I get into publishing?', what would you recommend? Can you think of the best, or in fact, the worst career
advice anyone has ever given you?**
I don't know that I have the dream job — just to focus on
that for a moment. I answer to the President, the Board,
committees and every single member of the Association. Some
people couldn't cope with the politics of doing that. Some
people prefer to work in a dedicated publishing company,
working on a project through to completion, having a distinct
line of authority within the firm. Personally, I love the politics
of working for every member of the Association. I love knowing what goes on in the industry, and I love working on the
range of issues that I do work on. So, my job is quite different
from most of those in the publishing industry. Quite often
people who come from publishing into this office don't enjoy
it, and they go back to publishing. People who enter the
industry via a job in this office then go on to work in
publishing, and take to those publishing companies a huge
range of qualifications and experiences that stand them in very
good stead.

**Plus, they would have a much broader knowledge of how the
whole industry works.**
Yes, that's right. Giving advice to people on how to enter the
industry — gosh! I try to find out what they're interested in,
and where their interest lies, and what they've done in the
past, and how that might assist them in getting a job in a
particular firm. Then, as we said earlier, tell them very quickly
what the pay rates are, because that will really focus their
minds. Many of them still have a romantic notion about the
industry, even after you've tried to dissuade them. They tend
to think that it's all cocktail parties, authors and overseas
bookfairs. It's not! So you see, I'll talk to them about where
their interests lie and, depending on their qualifications and
what they've studied, I'll tell them about the Macquarie and

Macleay courses in Sydney. If they're from Melbourne, I'll talk to them about the RMIT and Monash and other courses around, and Writers' Centres, if they're interested in that sort of activity. This can often fulfil a very useful role, particularly for would-be writers. Getting into the community of publishing — they can join Women in Publishing, they can join the Society of Editors and the Galley Club — so there's a strong networking bond that already exists for them to get in and meet people. They're not going to get in, probably, on their first job application. They should keep an eye on the arts pages of the *Sydney Morning Herald* for jobs, and in the positions vacant in the classifieds of the *Herald* and the *Age* and other newspapers around the country, although the bulk of publishing is located in Sydney and Melbourne. Increasingly, there are opportunities in Brisbane and Perth. So it's not just confined to the eastern seaboard. So you try and head them in the right direction, whilst also giving them a realistic view of just how challenging it can be. You try to encourage them to think about sales and marketing, not just editorial work. Not everybody is suited to that incredible detail required in editorial work. I personally think that marketing is a very stimulating area — you get to work on every title across the board, whereas editors only work on a selection of titles, perhaps in their subject range. Marketing, I think, can often be a very exciting area. Publicity and promotion, too, can really get you out among a lot more people. Women in particular have done extremely well across all these areas. Publishing is an industry in which women can do very well — sales, marketing, production, design, editing — all facets have been very attractive and very conducive to women.

The APA have their own publication don't they, *Introduction to Book Publishing*, which I believe is going to be updated?
Yes, we're working on updating it this year and early next year. The publication goes through all of the different divisions within a publishing house, perhaps concentrating on a larger house where there is a clearer division between editorial, design, production, sales, marketing, distribution, order fulfilment, management, and accounting, of course, and describes what each of these departments does for people. It's $5 and it's an invaluable guide for people who want to get an overview of the publishing industry. We also have snapshots of people who have done well in the industry across all of those different

working areas, and they give a bit of a background as to how they got into the industry, what their qualifications were or weren't, and what experiences they bring. Publishing is an entrepreneurial activity, and people who work in it often give very generously to the industry, and to the arts world all over. So you find people in publishing often sit on theatre boards or craft boards as well. They have a wide range of interests and when you're out there seeking new titles to have that broader range other than just books is terribly important. As we were saying earlier, it is a fashion led industry. We are as much drawn by fads and trends as the record, fashion and film industries. So knowing what's going on in those areas and being able to plug into the latest trends in film, for instance, or music, is terribly important. A very eclectic range of interests across all cultural activities is vital — doing things outside straight book publishing.

Otherwise you just hear your own point of view again and again.
Exactly. You do need to get out there and mix with young people, and people of all socioeconomic groups, and have a multicultural focus as well. It's not an industry in which you can just sit down and think, 'Oh yes, I'm going to work on this book'. You have to be concerned with what is going on in the community, and be a voracious reader of newspapers and magazines, and be a consumer of all popular culture.

18 Interview with Mersina Malakellis

Sales Representative and Key Accounts Manager, Random House Australia, Winner of the ABA Victorian Sales Representative of the Year Award 1995

Mersina, how did you become a sales rep rather than something else in publishing?
It was pure chance, believe it or not; I was working in a bookshop part-time, my studies were all in English Literature and I was working on a PhD at that time. I heard about a job going at Random (and these sorts of jobs are rare as hen's teeth), I applied and I got it, which was chance. In terms of targeting the publishing industry, I wouldn't really work for any other industry.

What makes the publishing industry so much better, or different to any other industry that you could have chosen?
The books! The product!

Are the people any nicer in publishing?
I think so, generally the people who work in publishing don't work there because they get well paid, they work very much because they love the environment, they love the product, which is a really terrible word for it, they love *books*, they love the personalities, they love the authors and it's worthwhile.

So, what do you think are the skills and abilities that make a good sales representative?
Rapport with your customers, a sensitivity to their needs, time efficiency (nobody wants their time wasted, least of all booksellers), knowledge, responsibility and follow-up service. So if

179

you say something is to be done, you make sure it is done. And commitment — all the things that make any job . . . anything that suits any career is relevant to the book trade, I mean I don't think there are any differences. You need to be a multi-faceted person and be able to deal with a wide range of people: booksellers, other sales reps and people within your company.

What is an example of a typical day for you?
Hectic! Four appointments usually, for myself geographically they tend to be centred in the city, so in terms of travelling around I don't have much of it, but it's hectic and the demands are greater the bigger the accounts. Today for example, I was in Myer Melbourne, the stock check took around three hours, the sell-in took about an hour, so there go four hours. On a day like this, I wouldn't even try to do four appointments. So it does vary according to the customers you see, but generally frantic, you may get half an hour for lunch!

When you started off working as a rep for Random, were you in the same territory doing the same job you're doing now?
No, I was a suburban rep. Nobody is allocated the city front up, you tend to work elsewhere for at least a year as far as I know. I worked the northern suburbs, the inner city and also the west when I first started.

Do you think it's different being a city rep as opposed to working in the suburbs?
Extremely. One is that the customers are much bigger; secondly they have quite a different business, they cater to quite a different market, so you need to know which books will suit them. They generally have a more independent market, they often have a very educated and business-oriented market. The quantities are so much bigger.

Are we talking double, triple, quadruple?
It's hard to say . . . probably quadruple for the major releases, so where you might get an order for twenty or so of a new hardback, one hundred is what you'd expect in a big city account — top authors here, we're not talking about the mid-list, but the difference is amazing. I spent the first three months closing my mouth, I couldn't get over the quantities.

And what do you think the advantages are between being a

sales representative, as you are now, over being a bookseller, as you were previously?
I can do a lot more with this job than I could as a bookseller. The marketing of certain titles is up to me, I can set up promotions whenever I like, there is a huge amount of autonomy, my time is my own. I obviously need to do certain things within that time, but how I allocate that time is up to me. A greater degree of specialist knowledge about books and what is working out in the marketplace. When you're working as a bookseller I think you tend to focus on what sells, but you don't have the overview. For example, I have an overview over eighty accounts, not just one. So I can see what trends are happening out there because my work allows me to see it. And that makes my knowledge of the book trade and titles that are likely to work, much better.

If someone said to you 'Mersina, I'd love to work in publishing', what could you recommend?
I think working as a bookseller is really the first step. The best publishers, the best editors seem to be the people who have done the whole thing: bookseller, rep, maybe management, sales, marketing or then diverting into the editing and publishing side. Knowing how the trade works is a major advantage when it comes to being a rep, there is a lot to know, it's a very specialised trade. The information you get as a rep is very helpful if you're going into publishing, as I was saying before, if you can pick the trends, then you can pick the winner.

Do people often say to you 'You're lucky to have a job that you love'?
All the time!

How do you see sales-repping helping your career in publishing progress? What's the next stage for you?
I see my role as a sales/marketing lifeline, and to this end I'm doing a little bit more further education, a post-graduate diploma in marketing. The experience I have on the coalface is seeing what works and what doesn't and that's not just my books, it's everybody really, checking out what Penguin are doing, what Pan Macmillan are doing, what HarperCollins are doing, seeing what works and *why*, and so that experience I'm gathering now. The other thing is dealing with all kinds of people, I can't stress enough what an asset that is. If I can deal with eighty-two personalities, then I figure that I've cov-

ered most of them. Honing people skills is the key, I think, to a career in publishing. It is a small industry in Australia and all the key players know each other. You cannot afford to not be a part of it, in a positive way.

What education have you done and how do you think it's been of assistance to you in your position as a sales representative? I have an Honours degree in English and I have a year and a half of a PhD under my belt, all in English literature. Obviously it's helpful to have a sense of the literary tradition, it's not important except for the independent accounts, it's important for book knowledge, I suppose, in general. I wouldn't say that my tertiary education has helped for a business environment, the other kind of work that I did was much more relevant, and that was in our family businesses, and having a practical head, I suppose. I'm also studying for a postgraduate diploma at RMIT and that's because I'm gearing myself towards a role in sales and marketing at a managerial level. There's my ambition!

19 Interview with Sue Hines

Publisher, Allen & Unwin

Sue, how did you get to be a publisher, was that your career ambition?

At eleven years of age adults would ask me the usual question, 'What are you going to be when you grow up?' Not quite knowing what a publisher did, beyond something with books, I would say with great confidence, 'I'm going to be a publisher'.

Somehow, twenty years later, I convinced Hilary McPhee and Di Gribble to take me on as their 'baby' editor. I'd been a teacher for years and by this time I was a senior teacher earning $28,000 a year. Working as an editorial assistant took my wage down to $16,000 per year — it was a serious decision. I have the usual English honours degree from Melbourne University, so I at least had that much of what it took. Three years later I was McPhee Gribble's managing editor. Eight months before it was sold to Penguin, I left to go to Reed. (I seem to have a sixth sense when it comes to takeovers.)

Traditionally Reed had been a hardback publisher and it was my job to establish a new paperback imprint in Australia. This wasn't as easy as it sounds because Reed wasn't sure what it had published. My way of finding books to turn into paperbacks was to go to the State Library and walk down the aisles looking for windmills on spines (i.e. the Heinemann colophon).

You're joking!
I found Randolph Stowe and Neville Shute . . .

Were the records so ambiguous?
They didn't exist. Reed was an old publishing house with the head office in London, and it had bought a few companies along the way and records had got lost in the takeovers . . . I went on to publish general non-fiction. Some of the non-fiction included a couple of illustrated books, you'd know them, probably — *New Food* and *Hot Food, Cool Jazz*. On the strength of that I became the illustrated books publisher, flying around the world selling co-editions and treading the tightrope of publishing coloured books in a tiny market. Nerve-racking but very exciting. It was an interesting career move, going from literary fiction — which is what McPhee Gribble did — through to non-fiction and then illustrated books. Reed, of course, is history now having been bought by Random House quite recently. I left in July last year, once again, just before the buy-out.

Do you play the stock market!?
No, but perhaps with that record I should! Now I'm building another list at Allen & Unwin, and I guess non-fiction is my thing: illustrated books, general non-fiction. I love reading fiction in my private life, but I don't particularly want to work in that area. That doesn't mean I won't do the odd novel here and there, but it's not my chosen path. The nice thing about being a publisher is that you can chart your own course, to some extent.

And what was the reality versus the fantasy, when you wanted to be a publisher and you went to McPhee Gribble?
I actually didn't want to be a publisher, I wanted to be an editor.

And what was editing like when you got in there and got down to it? Was it how you had expected it to be?
For the first three months I read the manuscript pile. Hilary said I wasn't allowed to read ten pages or fifty pages and just give up, I had to finish every single page. So for three months she sat me in front of the slush pile and I read. By the end of that time I knew exactly what was publishable and what wasn't. None of it was publishable and I knew every version of what was not publishable. Then I started proofreading

things that were publishable. McPhee Gribble was a small company and Hilary and Di did the editing. There was one other editorial assistant who'd been there longer than me, and we'd follow along behind Hilary and Di, just reading their editorial work and proofreading or whatever. That's pretty much what I thought an editor would do: take part in the process of crafting the country's literature.

I was being paid to have the arguments on behalf of the publishing house and to win those arguments in the interest of a better book. As I became a more proficient editor I realised that I had to act in the interest of the book without leaving the author feeling as though they'd lost control of their work. It's a fine balancing act. Editors need to be gentle but also they need to be pedantic control freaks: 'No you can't do this, you can put a verb there', and so on. I didn't expect that it would be such a job of negotiation and diplomacy. As an editor you are in a strange position. You have to protect the interest of the house while being the book's and the author's advocate within the publishing house.

I thought it was interesting the other night at the Galley Club when you mentioned that, when asked to describe their jobs, American editors use words like 'quarterback' and 'orchestra conductor', whereas in Australia editors use softer terms like 'handmaiden' or 'midwife'. Do you see yourself as a tyrant or are you more of a nurturer?
Well, you know a publisher's job and an editor's job are different ones; certainly in Australia they are. I think it is my job as publisher to make sure that people are happy and to protect the investment of the company . . .

Now when you say people, to whom are you referring?
The author: I think the author has to come out the other side of the publication process owning the book. They have to face the public holding their book on the Ray Martin Show, or wherever, on the radio, and they have to be able to say with no hesitation 'this book is mine'. But along the way, I have had to protect the interests and investment of the publishing house. I need to reassure the author of the expertise of the house, to give them sufficient confidence so that the author understands that this is an object which not only conveys the author's ideas faithfully, but it is an object which must be made attractive to the market. Sometimes these two interests are in

conflict. The author doesn't always understand that a book is a thing that has to be sold. As the publisher I share the author's interest in fidelity, but I have an additional need — I want to create a book for which the public will pay $50 and feel as though they've got value . . .

Value for money?
Yes, that, but also you may be buying a promise. Look at an interior design book, for instance, or a cook book where you may only make one recipe out of it but you love the book anyway, because the design is smart or it represents your style. These are the things that the publisher knows, but for the author the book is a way of putting their ideas in a concrete form, and so the enterprise is different for the two of us.

And what's a typical day in your professional life like? Is it all glamorous, running around in limousines with authors?
Of course [*laughing*]! Oh, there is some of that because there are a lot of famous people who want to write books, in fact the publisher chooses people who've got some sort of profile. In that way, you're a handmaiden to that person's fame. You don't share their fame, but you borrow from it as your job is to help create their book. But, I spend a lot of time with my authors and so sometimes great friendships develop. In a typical day I spend a lot of time on the phone.

Talking to authors?
Authors, but also to the rest of the publishing house wanting to know about the marketing for this or that book, to designers, to illustrators, to photographers, to freelance editors, to agents, to potential authors. Because I like design and I like the object of the book, I talk to designers myself. And photographers. I've always got time to see the work of designers and photographers, you never know when you'll find the next brilliant young artist, so you have to look. I don't deal with agents a lot because I tend to be a 'think-them-up-and-go-get-'em' kind of publisher, rather than waiting for books to come to me. There's a fair amount of keeping the show on the road, too. Take today, apart from my three appointments, I'll probably make twenty-five phone calls, many of them within the organisation itself. Can we call Joan Campbell's book *Bloody Delicious*? That was yesterday's drama. Ring the marketing director, can I call a book *Bloody Delicious*, what will the booksellers say, is it actually right for the book? I couldn't

write the catalogue copy until I had the title. At this stage the book doesn't actually exist, I'm the only one who has a clear idea of what the book is, so I'm writing the catalogue copy. I want everyone in the publishing house to be on side as well as the author. A lot of my time is spent talking to the publicity and marketing, and sales people and editors. Then there is the managing director, who is my boss after all, to be sure he is well informed, so that when the contract hits his desk he doesn't get a surprise.

Does that happen in other publishing houses?
No, it doesn't, but when you are outside the head office as I am, you've got to make sure that you've told the entire publishing house what's going on. You could easily forget to inform the rest of the chain. The publisher is the beginning of the chain, but it's company money I'm playing with, and not only that, the rest of the publishing house has got to market the book out to the world. The usual battle ground in a publishing house is the cover. I reserve the right to say what a cover is going to be but if someone in the house says they really hate that cover I have to pause and think about how well they will market a book if they hate the cover. In the end it's my decision. In that way I'm the quarterback kind of publisher that those American editors talked about. It is a matter of calming the rest of the company to make sure that they can own the decisions. And what else is in a day? . . . Oh, there's a lot of machinery and telephones and writing letters to people trying to convince them to do things that they may not have ever thought of doing before. Encouraging them and trying to give them the sort of confidence that enables them to write a book, dampening down the unrealistic expectations of authors, especially first-time authors. Most authors fly once they are published but some are terrified and then suddenly they feel that the world isn't taking the sort of notice that they had expected. I have so many high-profile authors, Jill Dupleix, Terry Durack, Max Walker, Gabriel Gaté, Charmaine Solomon. These are busy people in great demand and I have to ensure that each of them is sufficiently cared for and that their books are given the attention they need by the publishing house. I do care about them the way you care about . . . not exactly children, but it is that sense of different interests competing for my time. I care about the whole

publishing process, not just the editorial section. So that's what my day is, and then there's reading . . .

Reading! When do you have time to read?
At home. I spend two days working from home per week and on one of those I read. I divert the calls from home to the office and I don't answer the door and I don't answer the phone. If I wasn't tough about that, then I'd drown in manuscripts.

When people say to you, 'Sue, how do I get in, what should I put on my CV?', what do you tell them? What should they do or not do?
I think they should have organisational skills, but God only knows how you can tell when you're interviewing people; or, how they can exhibit organisational skills in an application? I don't know, but it seems to me, as an editor and as a publisher, that's the most important thing. You've got to be able to write, you've got to be literate, you've got to be numerate . . .

Numerate, as a publisher?
The bottom line is mine, on a book by book basis. If I don't set up each book to be profitable at the contract stage then what hope have we got of making a profit at the end of the day? You know, I had to learn how to do percentages on a calculator when I first started. I understand about costings, I know about overheads, I think publishers need to know how the finances fall. Each book has to pay its own way otherwise we won't be in business for long. I have to balance the cost of the photographer against the cost of the editing against the cost of the overhead, or whatever it is. So numeracy and literacy are important.

And professional diplomacy is important also. There may be people that you don't like, you're only dealing with them because it's your job. You're going to have to deal with requests that are unreasonable, demands that are actually impossible to juggle, and you've got to do it with some kind of enjoyment, and make the other person feel as if they have every right to make unreasonable requests of you. Basic people skills are essential.

And do you think people are better off doing some sort of

course, or having a good administrative background with a lot
of common sense?
Well, there are real skills needed for editing . . . how to spell,
and so on, but those skills are not very mysterious and can be
easily learnt and demonstrated. The mysterious stuff in editing
is all that business between the editor and the author, where
you are deeply engaged in trying to convince the author that
this is the best thing for their book and that they should do
as you suggest.

**What's the best career advice that you've ever heard, or that
someone has ever given you?**
This is something that I was told by someone who wasn't
actually in publishing. She said, 'Look at what the
organisation's strengths are'. If you find yourself in a publishing house that publishes educational books, don't do children's
books or mass market fiction. Look at the mainstream of what
the organisation does and you'll find the career path in there.
The career path is in the central skills that the organisation
has, as a corporate entity. Let's take Reed, as an example. Reed
was very good at commercial books — you know, Bryce
Courtenay and all that stuff. That organisation could do big
commercial books very well, and that's where their strengths
and interests lay. That influenced the kinds of books I published. I started to take on big names, big commercial books.
But the house had to be willing to take a few risks with these
authors and to spend some money in marketing and printing.
You can print 3000 copies of a book, or 30,000 copies, and
the effort for the publishing house is exactly the same. The
same amount of time goes into the publishing and editorial
end, at least. At McPhee Gribble, for instance, it would have
been stupid to take on those big commercial authors, because
that's not what they did well. Similarly they didn't produce
four-colour books, so cookbooks were out of the question. It's
good advice to look at what the organisation can do and tailor
your contribution to it. There is a chance then that the force
of the organisation will push you through the ranks, if you're
good at what you do. Stay with the skills of the organisation,
as well as your own skills. It's particularly good advice for a
woman as those further up the ladder are bound to be men.
So use the strong shoulders around you to help, don't be
crushed by them.

Have you heard any really dreadful advice, has anyone ever told you something that was just awful?
I think it's one of those safety devices that people have — you forget things that are not very helpful, don't you? I certainly wouldn't have listened to anyone who said, 'Don't buck the system.' The world does not profit from a whole lot of people who are jumping over the cliff together. It's the important other half of what I was just saying about going with the organisational flow, really.

If someone said to you, 'Wow! What you're doing is what I want to do', do you have any tips?
People who ring up saying they want to be an editor often mean I love reading novels and I want to turn my hobby into a career. Although I work in publishing, and being a reader is what took me into publishing, I actually read in a different way when I'm working to when I'm reading a blockbuster novel at the beach. I have different critical faculties switched on when I read for work to those I employ when I read for the sheer pleasure of it. It's the same as people thinking they can write a children's story because they were children once or because they have children. Or that because it's for kids it's easy. It's not, writing for children is the hardest thing in the world, and it's a particular skill that not everyone has.

You would get several CVs sent to you each week. Are there things you see on a CV that make you cringe?
Treat it like any other job. Think about your sense of what the task is, and then tell the employer how you can do that for them. I'm looking for an editor to employ right now. I have an editor already, and I really want a clone of her, I think.

So, what's so good about this person?
She's amazingly organised, she's terrifically diplomatic and wonderfully personable. She's also aware of the world — she reads, she looks, she sees; and she has a commercial sense. She doesn't say to me this book deserves to be published because it is a wonderful book. She says I think people will like this, and it will sell. She's got all of the skills that you need to craft the book as an editor, and she knows that the book has to reach an audience. Most people can spell, but not everyone has market sense. She's making decisions constantly and in all of those little decisions — even if she's just moving the commas around the manuscript — they're all about improving this thing

called the book so that it can find a purchaser and a reader. I look for someone who has an interesting life, who has a few things happening around them. It's not just about sitting at a desk; I look for people who've got a passion for something, I don't care what it is, whether it's gardening, skydiving or dogs — something! If they're connected to the world in some way, they're going to be a much better editor. But, if they're sitting at home doing nothing . . .

If you're out there doing something, you've presumably got a lot of energy as well.
Give the task to someone who's already got too much to do. People who are busy achieve more. Some people can make a meal out of the simplest task. If you give it to a busy person, they don't have time to muck around on the edges and worry about it — they'll just do it. I'm looking for editors who are plugged in to the world, for whom work is one interesting strand in a busy and interesting life.

20 Interview with Robert Coco

Publishing Manager, Pearson Professional

Robert, how did you get into publishing?
Like most people it was chance. I was quite young when the opportunity to work with the Australian Government Publishing Service was presented to me. It was my second job after working at Channel Nine, and when the position came up, I simply took it. I had no expectations of the publishing industry or any vision of developing a publishing career.

The work you're doing at the moment, you are the publisher, the buck stops with you, what's a typical day like, is it very glamorous?
The short answer is no. I think if you're outside the industry, people view it as glamorous, but if you work inside it, you realise it's a business like any other business, and the business is there to make a profit for the owners. You've got a number of key stakeholders and you have to balance their needs, so it's very much a working day just as it is in any other industry. I don't see my segment of the market as glamorous, although there is a distinction between different segments in the industry. I work in a professional publishing environment which, when compared to the trade, for example, would be considered less glamorous. I think if you asked a trade publisher if it was a glamorous industry, they might have a different opinion.

When you started off at AGPS, what were you doing there?
I was bookselling. At that time, the AGPS list consisted mainly

192

of legislation and reports. It was a good reason to get out of bookselling and into publishing.

So how do you get from being a bookseller to being a publisher?
Well, that was an accident too! There was a break in between the AGPS and publishing. From the AGPS, I went to the Royal Commission of Inquiry into the Federated Ship Painters and Dockers Union, which once again was a shift into left field, except that I had an interest in research. I got a training opportunity in the research area and that was the beginning of a commercial career for me, initially involving analysing the activities of companies involved in illegal activities. From there, I went on to work with the National Crime Authority in a similar role. A couple of years later, I re-entered the publishing industry by applying for a job as an editor with a business publisher. The role was to edit *The Australian Public Companies Guide* and my claim to fame was that I predicted a fall in the stock market in 1987. True. Just look up the May newsletter. My previous experience in researching companies and following the flow of illegal funds was a good grounding for the study of publicly listed Australian companies!

And at the moment you're doing an MBA, what sort of subjects are you doing?
I'm doing 'managing people' and 'accounting and financial management' subjects this semester.

Do you feel that what you're studying has direct application to what you're doing on a day-to-day basis?
There's no question about it. What they teach you in the MBA is to apply the theory to the workplace. That is the fundamental basis of the course — there are few case studies given to you — the case studies are drawn from your own workplace and it is really interesting to get the views of your fellow sufferers on your set of problems. I'm the only publisher doing the course as far as I am aware, so the solutions can be quite innovative.

What do you think about the sudden proliferation of publishing courses? People like you and I got into publishing one way or another, but now the industry has tightened up, there are

lots of publishing courses around. **What do you think about people doing those instead of gaining experience?**
Both are important, but I think the courses are fantastic to be perfectly honest because you can build knowledge and skills in a much shorter period of time than you would be able to in the workplace. In the MBA, you cover a whole range of different subjects over a three-year period — managing people, marketing, total quality management, business strategy. Similarly, through the publishing courses, you get exposed to editorial, production, sales and marketing, finance and general publishing practices.

And do you get many people ringing you up saying, 'Robert, I'd love a job in publishing, how do I get in?'
Heaps!

And what sort of advice do you give, what do you tell them?
Well, the first piece of advice I give them is to do a course. The reason for this is that the benchmark has been raised now with a number of courses being offered, whereas there were no formal courses when we came through. Before these courses commenced around 1990 I think, you would take anybody that had an arts degree or something similar and that would be your safest option. You would pick from that group of people. Nowadays, with people having gone through those courses and achieving a specific publishing industry qualification, this is the benchmark. The people who are trying to enter the industry without this type of qualification are competing against those that have got one. If they're really serious about getting a position in the industry, they have to show their commitment by completing, or at least starting a course.

And, what do you think about the people coming out of those courses? Do you get people applying to your company directly who have done those courses?
Interestingly enough, no.

Why? Is that because professional publishing is perceived very differently?
I think that's right. I think a lot of people coming out of the course are focused on the 'sexier' segments of the publishing industry and professional publishing may appear to them to be a bit dour, so they're going for the trade where there's the opportunity to work with high-profile authors, the media and

that kind of thing. They miss out because they fail to appreciate thrills such as winning a competitive tender, or getting ten per cent response to a direct marketing campaign. I know this sounds really sad, but this is what publishing does to you.

So do you think that perhaps it's because they're not exposed to professional publishing in the courses, or is it really a hidden publishing segment?
I don't know the answer to that. I'd be surprised if professional publishing got much exposure in the courses.

I mention it in my course because I've done work in that area myself. But I think too many students seem to be very interested in, as you said, the sexy side, the trade side, the stuff they see every day in the bookshops.
Absolutely, yes. Professional publishing is essentially a part of the information industry — we sell information to a professional audience, we don't have a high public profile like the Penguins and Macmillans.

What's the best publishing career advice anyone has ever given you?
Get out there and network. Also, be proactive about getting your name in front of as many people as possible, any way you can. If you are a marketing person responsible for direct mail, make sure that you send your direct marketing pieces to every marketing manager in the industry — and do it in a subtle way by simply adding the names on to the back of a regular mailing. Don't send a covering letter announcing how fantastic you are 'as can be judged by these superb examples'. If you want a particular job, make sure that the people who make the decisions know of you. In my case, Kerry Packer gets a letter from the publisher every week!

Well, have you ever been given any really terrible career advice?
Actually, any kind of career advice has been infrequent. You really need to seek it out, which means finding a mentor or a professional career manager.

How many books a year do you oversee as publisher coming out of Pearson Professional?
Well, last year we did about 25 books and loose-leaf manuals, plus half a dozen newsletters and two electronic publications.

And what would the print run of those be?
It would vary, but around about 1500–2000 print run. That's
a typical professional publishing print run for a book. You
need to remember that some of this product is relatively
expensive. We might only print 500 loose-leaf manuals first up
at $250 rrp.

Which has got a much smaller market than the trade area?
Yes, a completely different financial profile — smaller runs,
considerably higher prices, a lot of marketing through non-
retail channels.

**And what's the best thing about being a publisher as opposed
to being a bookseller or an editor?**
The work variety, and particularly dealing with authors who
can be anything from fantastic self-promoters and terrific
people through to real prima donnas. But it's about exposure
to a broad range of tasks dealing with every aspect of the
company's activities. You've got to be in touch with the
market, so you talk to booksellers, professional associations,
the media, government agencies, managers and academics.

Within the organisation, you have to work with sales and
marketing, on the finance side with the accounts people, with
editors and designers in production, and management on the
strategic development of the business. It's a total relationships
position, and you have to manage all those relationships.
That's what I like about it. It sounds clichéd, but it's the wide
range of people you deal with.

I often comment to people that the role of the publisher
carries with it a special status that allows me to open most
doors within my market segment. People don't feel threatened
by a publisher because they are not perceived to be selling
anything. They are usually curious to know why I might be
contacting them.

What else do I like about it? I love publishing successes,
no doubt about that.

**And when you're interviewing people for positions, is there
anything you really hate people doing in interviews or application letters? And have you got any suggestions for what
people should be doing when they're applying for a position
with a professional publisher?**
What I like to see is someone who not only understands the
position but more importantly, can articulate how they will

add value to our business. Anyone that does a little research about our company, our competitors and what they would do if they had the job is streets ahead of a less prepared applicant. The other suggestion I would have is to make the written application stand out by not just sending the usual one page covering letter followed by three pages of CV. Be creative with the packaging or the contents so that the employer can see some initiative. What's the application for?

Say for an editorial position — they're telling me in their covering letter that they want to be an editor but I read their CV and I see them coming across as a writer. They are giving me a mixed message, so there's no way I'm going to put them up for an editorial position because I know they want something else and there will be a problem there.
It's a kind of a backdoor way of trying to get their stuff published, isn't it?

Well, for example, a marketing manager I know hired the woman who is her publicist not just because she was a great candidate, but because she was also the only person in the interview who said, 'I want to be a publicist'. This candidate didn't want to be an editor and when the Marketing Manager said, 'What do you want to do in five years' time?', she said, 'I want to be Publicity Manager'. There was consistency there in her whole approach to the job. I interview people every week and they're telling me one thing and generally, they want something quite different and I find that quite frustrating as an interviewer. Do you have similar things happen when you're interviewing people because of the nature of your area of publishing being so specialised, are they very much more focused on what they want to do?
They are. Anybody that applies for a job with our organisation has got to have some kind of business interest or business focus, there's no question about that. So, in a way, that can preclude a lot of people from the general publishing industry applying. For example, when we had our legal publishing operations, we needed a managing editor who was also a lawyer, so that cut out many of those editors that could have applied. We require specialists, and not just publishing specialists — specialists in specific disciplines with publishing experience.

Is that because you feel you can teach them the publishing process, but not the other?
We'd like both, but it's very difficult to get both. If it came to a choice, we'd probably go for the person with the specialist experience and teach them the publishing side of it, but it does depend on the position. Certainly not in the case of a managing editor. For example, the person we had last year (as managing editor) had 15 years' experience in publishing, as well as legal qualifications with legal practice experience. We had to have a lawyer, but we couldn't have taken anyone without a solid editorial background. We had a lot of trouble replacing her when she left.

And do you see professional publishing going towards more on-line and electronic publishing?
Absolutely. Professional publishing — particularly reference publishing — will go on-line. The segment of the professional business publishing that will stay in print are the business books; there will always be a print market for that type of publication, however, business information that changes rapidly will go on-line. That is a lot of money that will transfer from the print to the electronic medium. CD-ROMs will not have the impact that some people are talking about. The information can be downloaded from the net and the speed increases every month.

Do you feel that there will be a publishing on-demand situation versus producing large print runs, having them sitting in the warehouse waiting to be sold rather than having the electronic product available?
Most of it will be on-line — we are developing a publishing database that people can hook into and pull out the information they want on a subscription basis. That is the future for the professional publisher — if you look at some of these publishers, the lion's share of their revenues are subscription-based, information services. That is how many people will obtain their professional information in the future, from an on-line service on the Internet. We are also producing print-on-demand products using docutec technology, but this is mainly for non-updating manuals.

Any other advice to people wanting to break into publishing?
Those people trying to get in for the first time should take whatever they can get. It's a small industry and you get a lot

of people saying, 'I want to be an editor', but even if you've gone through a course and got the relevant qualification, take what you can get as a starting point and then move towards your goal. Some people will take the high moral ground and say, 'If I'm not going to be offered a job as an editor, then I'm not going to do it'. To me, that's crazy. They have to get real and say I've got to get down from there and be a secretary, a receptionist, a sales person, a store person whatever. It won't do them any harm and eventually they will be able to move into that editorial stream, for sure. You have to get into the industry any way you can and once you're in, you can move around. The industry is fantastically networked, so once you are in through the door, the biggest obstacle is out of the way.

21 Interview with Alison Baverstock

UK Freelance Marketing Consultant and Author

How did you get started in your publishing career?

I can be a creature of impulse. In my last year at university I was heading towards a career in museums, then I overheard (in the Christmas holidays) a fellow student talking about how she had been working for her father's literary agent. She turned out to be the daughter of a well-known author. I thought it sounded fascinating, so I dug around a bit to find out about publishing, discovered Unwin's *Truth about Publishing,* and then I decided that that was what I was going to do — I was going to be a publisher. In those days there were very few graduate traineeships, you did a secretarial course to get in. I very firmly didn't want to do a secretarial course; having spent four years paddling my own canoe at university, so I decided to look for something related to publishing.

I got a job with a direct marketing firm called IBIS, who dealt with a lot of publishers. This was a brilliant place to start, direct marketing was then in its infancy and now it's become a really key area — you need to know about direct marketing to do almost anything, really. This was also an excellent place from which to be thinking about a job in publishing. I was dealing with lots of different publishers, selling them IBIS's services, and I got to see a lot of different standards and styles in publishing and think very clearly about where I wanted to end up. The other thing it did was toughen me up a bit. Knocking IBIS was an industry hobby; the publishing industry was very unused to direct marketing and IBIS was professional in the way they offered their services. The publishing industry rather looked down on them, but I found the sales training and the hands-on marketing experience to be an excellent grounding for a career in marketing in publishing.

You have written two books: *How to Market Books*, now in it's second edition, and *Are Books Different?*.
I must say immediately that I don't have a professional marketing qualification. I think that there is an awful lot of jargon in marketing that often theorises the obvious — all those complicated names and phrases for things that are really quite straightforward. It struck me from research that a completely jargon-free book of marketing might be useful, hence my third title, *Commonsense Marketing for Non-marketeers: A jargon-free guide*.

How long have you been working as a marketing consultant?
After about eighteen months with IBIS, I got a job with one of my customers, Heinemann Educational. This was quite an exciting time to be there because they were just starting to publish educational computer software. I then went to Macmillan and did several things for them. When you start climbing the tree in publishing you spend your life in meetings and I grew to loathe them. I found I was commissioning-out the copywriting because I didn't have time to do it, although it was the part of the job I most enjoyed. The freelance option seemed obvious and I started out as a copywriter. This is a very privileged position, because a copywriter does all the research and is in a very good place to make suggestions about the overall marketing–promotional plan and so on. I got myself listed in a directory of freelance copywriters and from there my name was picked up by the CEO of Book House Training Centre who needed teachers for copywriting courses. Although I had done no teaching before, I found it was something that I adored doing. Writing is a very solitary pursuit and so to spend a few days every couple of months enthusing at people is something I very much enjoy. I've been teaching for 8 or 9 years now. I don't do too much of it, because if you are

teaching you have to be up to date with what is happening in the industry. Also without new examples to refer to, I think I would start to bore myself.

The first book, *How to Market Books,* came to life because Dag Smith asked me to provide a handout for the course and I didn't know where to stop! There seemed to be so many ideas worth passing on. I think that publishers have always relied on the fact that they employ bright people and don't spend too much time explaining industry practice. I know that when I got the first job, there were so many things that I was assumed to know and I didn't like to ask. I consequently spent ages reinventing the wheel. If someone had just taken the trouble to explain how things worked, it would have saved so much time and money. So what started as a handout became the book that I would have liked when I started out in publishing. We did a revised edition in 1993 and it's now in its second edition.

With the regular work you do, apart from writing books, you also run training seminars for the Book House Training Centre?
Yes, that's rather fun, because they come up with a theme and it's up to me to get the speakers and devise the program. I get a lot of satisfaction out of putting together different types of personalities, voices and perspectives to create an event that other people will enjoy attending.

Do you have many people coming up to you saying, 'You are so lucky to work in publishing' or 'How do I get in?'?
At parties I find that if you mention you work in publishing everybody's eyes light up; they imagine that you spend your life lunching bestselling authors. Well, I work in the non-sexy end of publishing: mostly direct marketing for business or professional publishers. I fax copy backward and forward to the client; and work the same way with designers and printers — we seldom meet up. But it's true that there is a real mystique about getting into publishing. I think it's largely misplaced; those who do work in publishing have not found it that difficult to get a job. Understanding that it might be hard can put people off trying which does separate the sheep from the goats! Perseverance gets you in.

When I decided to go into publishing, I read everything I

could about the industry, including the *Bookseller*, and I think that will always encourage potential employers to consider you.

Do you work on your own?
Well, I tend to keep a balance, as copywriting is a very solitary pursuit and I like to keep in contact with other people. I very much enjoy training as the students are so enthusiastic. I have also found that my books have led to some marketing and management consultancy jobs. And there are requests from students who are studying for help with their projects. I don't mind if people ring me up and ask me questions, I do ask a lot of publisher friends to check my new material, so I feel that it is only fair that people can ask me for help. But I don't respond terribly well if they write and say please do my project for me! At the moment I am working on a correspondence course on copywriting and I am doing this in collaboration with the person I teach the copywriting course with.

I still find publishing hugely exciting. I love the way an idea becomes a book. The people are also very nice. I was asking a designer the other day why she worked mostly in publishing. Her response was, 'I know I'll get paid'! Publishers tend to be quite ethical and honourable. It's interesting that publishers tend not to industry hop — it's very civilised; an industry with a good public image.

In the future I'd like to do more of the same. As regards having a permanent job, I love my freedom and the variety of what I do so much. The books have led to many interesting opportunities, lots of travelling, I've been invited to speak overseas. I want to do more teaching and to write some fiction, in the hope that it is easier to get published if you have a couple of other titles in print.

I don't work full time, I work part-time. I think this is important. I have time to look at what other people are producing and to consider the huge variety of consumer choice. I think too, as a publishing marketeer, we have to be very aware of the marketing stimuli that other organisations are sending out. As I wander around supermarkets, buy petrol and so on, I absorb marketing stimuli in lots of different situations and get inspired by other peoples' direct marketing.

Do you feel you have adequate compensation?
Firstly, I'm lucky to be able to work freelance. Publishing has always had a tradition of relying on people outside the office,

such as freelance editors, designers and readers — this is a
huge opportunity. I don't know many freelance bankers. My
books have raised my profile and led to interesting jobs. You
asked about the glass ceiling, but I think publishing is a good
industry for women — there are more and more women at
director level and running their own businesses, we definitely
do better than in lots of other industries. It is true that
publishing is quite cliquey and in the past has been inward-
looking. But I sense that a breath of fresh air is sweeping
through the industry. When I started the collective view of
marketing was as being rather vulgar. I remember when I
resigned from my job in the marketing department of an
educational publisher the managing director gave me an interview and waved several marketing-based carrots in front of me
to encourage me to stay. I kept saying no and then he finally
said, 'OK, we'll make you an editor' which I thought was really
funny! Most of the CEOs now are marketeers not editors and
the old fuddy duddys are mostly gone. When I started in
publishing we weren't allowed to write the promotional copy
— that was seen as an editorial job. These days marketing is
seen as a really positive thing, in career focus you are better
off with a marketing than an editorial background. We are
seeing more and more companies that are marketing, rather
than editorial led, which was not the case when I joined the
industry.

**Where do you see the industry going in the next four or five
years?**
I think that it is both frightening and challenging! Knowledge
of how publishing works is no longer a guarantee of success.
There are firms outside of publishing who are looking at
publishing as an opportunity — like the Disney Corporation.
For example, a well-known British firm called Batsford, which
published books on chess, bridge and crafts, was bought by a
media group only three years old (about 18 months ago). On
the other hand there are other organisations who are starting
to publish from scratch (mainly the organisations selling
through supermarkets). They used to buy publishers' books
and sell them there, and they are now publishing them themselves. So other people are now looking at publishing and
thinking there is money to be made, how do I get in there?
This gets back to marketing. Publishers who are streetwise,

will do very well, those who are not will most likely go to the wall or be bought up.

Where should you start your career in publishing?
Most graduate entrants want to be editors. I think people have this ivory tower image, that if you are editor nobody can bother you; you sit in your office all day and read beautiful prose. But the best editors these days are people who understand the market and can create a book or product for a specific niche. It is very interesting that at one stage it was assumed you would start as a copy editor, and then progress to be commissioning editor. But you have to understand you now see adverts (in the UK) for commissioning editors who don't have any editing experience at all. Today it's vital for everyone to understand how marketing works and how products are created: how to spot market niches.

I also think a marketing job is more fun! There are so many new ways of marketing today. For example, showing videos of books to children often validates the process of reading. A lot of children see a character on TV, they see the video and *then* ask for the book (I know that purists will be horrified). In the past, British publishers have always concentrated on the wealthier and better-educated end of the market and ignored the rest. But today marketing-aware publishers are selling huge quantities of more popular material. I think the most useful commodity for the future is enthusiasm. And there is nothing more inspiring than being in a bookshop and someone saying, 'Well, if you enjoy that, you'll enjoy this', it gives the customer confidence to buy.

22 Interview with John Curtain

Associate Professor of Publishing Studies,
Department of Communication Studies, RMIT

How long have you been in publishing?
33 years! I came into publishing through editorial. I had been a teacher during which time I had become secretary of the English Teachers Association, and started a journal, *English in Australia*, which is still going. Andrew Fabinyi who was at Cheshire employed me with the title 'Educational'. John Hooker was senior editor with Sandra Forbes and Noel Goss, so I was there to help look after schools publishing. I was at Cheshire for about five years, and I became publishing manager of Cheshire within the Cheshire Group after Andrew Fabinyi left. It was an interesting time because Lansdowne Cheshire, Sun Books and the bookshops were part of the group when Brian Stonier was Managing Director. I later worked for John Murray and W&R Chambers in the UK and managed Lansdowne Press and Richmond Hill Press when we returned to Australia. Before coming to RMIT, I was non-fiction publisher at Penguin Australia.

How did you become involved in the RMIT course?
I became involved when they advertised the position and I applied eight years ago. Before then, the course had been going for two years: one year full-time with 12 students and one year part-time with 25 students. The Society of Editors were really the inspiration, about ten years earlier, for this course. There was a lot of early discussion with people like Ruth Dixon and Anne Godden; later, enthusiasts, such as Teresa Pitt and Colin

Jevons, made it happen. When it was set up for the first year it was full-time, so they didn't take people from the book trade. But the Society of Editors felt that what they wanted was a course that would train people who were already working in publishing. So, when I came, we inherited the second year and brought in a new first year, so we had 25 students in each of the two years of the course. We had lots of applications from a whole range of people, but after a couple of years we were getting more applications from the publishing industry. It seemed that (a) we are keeping faith with the industry and (b) people were working better if they had access to the synergy of working with people back at work and with each other.

So, because we had so many applicants for the course (200 to 300 applicants for the 25 places), it seemed better to use as one of the criteria, experience in the industry. We define it loosely as 'experience or interest in'. What the future may bring as the fees go up and as a result of government policy is yet to be seen.

We have changed the course quite a bit from its purely editorial bias, adding in the second year a concentration on the business of publishing. So I suppose that the major changes in the course have been the development of this emphasis on business; the development of a subject on electronic production (production for the web, CD-ROM and multi-media); and the extension of the range of applicants from editorial through sales, marketing, bookselling, customer service, and production. The range of interests the students provide makes discussion much more stimulating and therefore better informed.

We aim to help students work out whether they want to be in the industry, and, if they do, in what area they would contribute best and gain most satisfaction.

Applicants and students feel some stress at the changes in the trade. A basic uncertainty stems from the crucial changes brought about by the digital revolution; another source of anxiety comes as companies are realigned in new alliances and specialisations, generally managed from overseas, thereby affecting the continuance of jobs and their availability.

I think that students who can embrace the potential of the technological changes and see how their jobs can adapt will be successful. Students who maintain standards of quality, imagination and an eye for detail will enjoy the book trade whether their products are print or electronic.

The technological changes have given younger people a remarkable opportunity for contributing to publishing, because, in many cases, they are more familiar with the technology than those older and more senior in the trade. We are in a rare era where the learning needs to go up from the young to the old, as those with long experience in the traditional book industry may find themselves knowing less about its potential than those who are entering it.

Index